SWEAR at YOUR BUSINESS

... it helps!

**Owners & Managers
Guide to surviving
Your Business**

RAY PEDERSEN

Other books in this series:

SWEAR at Your Business
For Owners & Managers
Your business is not the entity you work for, but that part of it you are responsible for.

SWEAR at Your Staff
For Team Leaders
Team Leaders control the people who create the income, expenses and the profits!

SWEAR at Your Customers
For Sales, Marketing & Customer Service
Businesses can survive without a manager, an accountant or a receptionist for a time; but what business cannot survive without, is sales!

© Copyright: 2010 RayPedersen

Ray Pedersen
www.RayPedersen.net
PO Box 223, Coolangatta Qld 4225, Australia

Includes revised editions – 2003, 2005, 2008
Cartoon permission by Brian Zaikowski www.bztoons.com

Disclaimer: The information in this book has been prepared solely for the purpose of information and guidance and is intended for the use of the recipient only. Its contents are covered by Copyright © of the author, including permission where applicable for illustrations, diagrams etc and may be legally privileged. Any disclosure, copying, distribution or any action taken or omitted to be taken in reliance on it, is prohibited and may be unlawful.

Did you go into business to keep losing money until you finally went broke?

No, you went into business with the simple idea to offer a great product or service and enjoy financial independence from it ... right?

Or maybe you took that management role to make a difference to the Company and improve your lifestyle?

So how come now you're up to your neck in problems, chasing banks and customers for money; and changing the photo on your desk every few months so you know what your family looks like?

Is running Your Business really that much harder than you thought?

You probably know there are a mountain of books, seminars and advisors out there to help you answer that; and if you've already tried them you'll know the problem is that each book and seminar gives you different advice and different ideas to follow. That's because the people offering these ideas all come from different career backgrounds with different approaches to solving business problems.

Unfortunately, and this is the real problem - each piece of advice CAN and WILL (probably) help you ... if it is right for your business and ... if you apply it the right way ... and at the right time.

SWEAR at Your Business helps you understand your business better, to know what is *right* for you and more importantly, to recognise the *right time* to use that inform or idea!

Written for the owner and/ or manager who controls a business or a part of one ... and who wants to know:
- How to simplify Your Business ...
- How to understand it better ...
- How to make it more successful, and ...
- How to enjoy it more!

Your Business
Is not the enterprise
You work for or own
... It is the part that you control*!*

How well do you control Your Business?

Contents

BEFORE YOU BEGIN THIS BOOK
        About SWEAR at Your Business   7
        A Message to Garcia   18

1. The first lesson in business   28
2. Simplifying Your Business   32
3. KISS   35
4. UNDERSTAND   39
5. PAL   44
6. Staff – your number 1 liability   48
7. Your Business Reputation   56
8. Your Company Culture   59
9. Marketplace, the factor beyond your control   62
10. Managing the Liabilities – Part 1   66
11. Managing Liabilities – Part 2   78
12. Your Business Model   89
13. Delegating   101
14. Using Reports   106
15. Growing Your Business – Part 1   110
16. Growing Your Business – Part 2   125
17. Keeping Your Business   133
18. Growing Yourself   140
19. Final Thoughts   152
20. DIY – Business Needs Analysis   156

BEFORE YOU BEGIN THIS BOOK
About SWEAR

SWEAR at your Business will help you handle the processes and people that work in Your Business - a set of tools, proven over many years and based on the fundamentals of Business Systems Engineering

"Hang on!" I hear you asking "What makes this any different to all the other management books?"

SWEAR at Your Business is about understanding Your Business – what is happening now, and why - it is easy to read and even easier to apply and best of all you'll be able to use it and see the benefits from day one!

Let's take a quick look at what is behind SWEAR at Your Business to show you why it fits for you.

As you've probably guessed SWEAR is an acronym, and we'll look at what the letters stand for later, but for now, ask yourself "Why do we swear?"

'We usually swear because someone or something has gone wrong and the outcome has made us angry; and now what we want is for the problem to be fixed, and preferably, so that it will not happen again!'

As business leaders we can all relate to this because from time to time things do go wrong; so I'd say it's a fair bet that many of us swear, some of us more than others.

The fact is that if you want to stop these *problems* from happening you know that you'll have to make changes to something – but what?

I'll stick my neck out here and suggest you may have already tried changing 'this' and found that you had to change 'that' as well; and after a few more changes to other things the program still didn't work effectively. And to make matter worse the problem reappeared … and this lead to more swearing, right?

Maybe it's time for a fresh look at things?

Would it help if you could simplify your business and know how to improve processes and manage things without always having to put out fires?

Would it help if you knew some tricks about making things more efficient? Like how to fix problems in a way that stops them from happening again? How to deal with staff more effectively? How to make Your Business more productive and how to make it more enjoyable for you?

You've got it!

What we're going to do is ... simplify Your Business by breaking it down into small easy to understand parts and show you how all the parts work and interact with each other ...from this you will see why problems happen, how to fix them and exactly what to do to prevent them from happening again ... no more next times!

SWEAR at Your Business Housekeeping rules.

Before we start we need to do a bit of housekeeping - you know tidy up and get rid of unwanted stuff – this housekeeping will show you how and why SWEAR works for YOU.

For a start, *Your Business* is not the enterprise that you work for - it's that part of it that you are responsible for. So if you are the CEO, or a sole-trader, then *your business* might well be the whole show; but if you're a Manager, Supervisor or Lead Hand then the division, department or project and the people that you personally (try to) control is *Your Business*.

Secondly, do you, like most business leaders have problems with staff, and think that your problems are new or unique - the result for your individual way of doing business? Nothing could be further from the truth. People are people and they have similar dreams, expectations and flaws from one generation to the next. Ask yourself, what do you want from life, or expect from your job, and what about that is so very different to your father, or the guy next door?

It is because of these similarities that staff related problems have not changed much over a hundred years or more. Sure, as Your Business grew you got more problems – more people create more problems, a smarter more tech-savvy workforce demand more because they understand the rules better; new technology may cause different versions of old issues that have to be addressed. But the causes of the problems are the same - always have been and always will be – everyone has always wanted more pay, less work, a better future and to be not responsible if trouble starts!

To help you appreciate how much things have **not changed** over the years I have included a copy of a newspaper article written in 1899 (that's right well over a hundred years ago), it's called 'A Message to Garcia' and it looks at the 'staff' problems faced by business owners of that day. I promise you will recognise the issues, infact many of you will think the article was written about your staff today.

Thirdly, what you (already) know is important, because that is what you base your answers and directions on. Unfortunately this is the proverbial two-edged sword (it cuts both ways) because all of us are limited by what we know and what we don't know. To understand this, imagine if you are in a sinking boat and someone, whom you know can't swim wants to jump in and go for it; you would stop them, for their own sake, right? But imagine if you're in that boat and you don't know that you can't swim – you'd probably jump in with them.

So the problem with basing your decisions on 'your prior knowledge' is that they can be limited, not just by what you know, but also by the things you don't even know that you need to know!

Think back over the recent past, how many times has 'Oops' been something that you said to yourself because you didn't have all the facts that you needed about the issue before you answered?

Clearly it would help if your knowledge had ALL the experience of others who have 'been there and done that' or if you had a checklist to make sure that you knew what you needed to know. That way you could manage the people, the problems and the risks that you face in business everyday … with confidence!

Lastly, a key lesson in SWEAR at Your Business is that you should challenge all information given to you, no matter where it comes from; to test if it is right for you. So, as your first lesson you should start by challenging the information being offered in SWEAR so you can understand where it comes from and if it is right for you?

About the Author

I have spent over thirty years supervising, managing and consulting to businesses large and small; many in labour intensive industries like contract and labour hire, manufacturing, retail and commercial sales, restaurants/ catering businesses, mining, automotive and light engineering, construction, sports management, etc. I actually started in the 1970's as a Systems Analyst, preparing (and designing) business processes to be handled by computer (no plug & play, no CD; these were the days of main frames with punch cards etc) and, as is the way of all good stories, my career path took me along a few twists and turns.

I will touch on some of these real-life adventures at times throughout this book but the main benefit to you (in my story) is that I have spent tens of thousands of hours observing the problems that business' face (and often create); and the solutions they have tried when handling them. From this and many more hours of study has evolved a series of basic laws (things you have to know) and simple steps (things you have to do) to correct these problems by better directing the efforts of those involved.

SWEAR at Your Business then gives you these laws and the steps, without the thousands of hours of learning; all based on the examples of others. Sort of like exam cheat sheets – all the answers and the reasons why, without the stress!

Rather than bore you with pages of what I have done and who I've done it for (yawn); I thought it would be more helpful for you to see some of their problems and the answers and let you compare how these solutions may match your needs!

One of the more interesting observations is that – 'the same situations cause the same problems in totally diverse businesses, time and time again!'

> **Challenge:** Have you ever had to address an earlier problem?
> A:

This is a real challenge for all business leaders but fixing this is not as hard as you may think as we'll see in later chapters.

By the way speaking of challenges, get used to facing them, as they appear throughout this book to help you recognise the problems that affect Your Business; and how the answer can make the difference between success and failure. Write your answers to each in the box and re-visit them later to see how much your approach is evolving.

Another common problem I hear is 'if only I had more reliable staff?' Some people say it every day, others many times every day. How about you?

Staff problems will affect everything in Your Business because everything in business relies on people to do it, or to make sure it is done!

To help improve your people management – skills and abilities of you and your Team Leaders - may I suggest you read **SWEAR at Your Staff**, the how, to and why book of being a better Team Leader.

Earlier I mentioned 'A Message to Garcia' and how it addresses the issues of employing staff; well, it also makes you think about what type of employees you want to have? And, what type of employee you are?

My second challenge therefore is -

> **Challenge:** How reliable is your staff? How reliable are you?
> A:

I know many of you may be thinking 'I've read stuff like this before' or 'I've tried this and it didn't work with my staff' and my response to that is 'So try it again?'

When did you try it? How did you apply it? Did anyone 'need' or 'want to know' what you were saying at that time?

People are funny. We will only respond to an idea when we have the need or can see the advantage (to us). We all want to know how the idea or plan fits our needs, and benefits us! And we will not respond to an idea (favourably) or try any idea unless we do. To put this another way –

"You can lead a horse to water but you can't make it drink ... until it wants to"

Just like that horse, your staff will only respond when you create the 'want' and when they can see what's in it for them! And, just like that horse, you will only consider applying this information when you can see the need - understand how it works and see what's in it for you!

So, what we have to do is make you want to read on, because, based on what I've just said, if you don't 'want' this info now – then you won't read it now, which means you won't know it and you can't apply it when you do need it!

Sometimes you don't know what it is that you need to know ... until it's too late! Remember being in that boat – do you want to drown?

I once worked with a Company that closed down a project in which they had already invested a year, not to mention a lot of money; only to watch it make millions of dollars for a competitor ten months later. Why? Because the decision makers did not know what they didn't know; they didn't 'understand' the situation (in this case that their prospective clients were of a type that needed a full financial year to assess, decide to buy and then budget the purchase) and they allowed good advice (to give it another year) to fall on deaf ears.

Simply, they scrapped the project because after a year they had no sales and no orders. The idea that clients needed more time didn't 'click'. Of course, when it did eventually click it was too late and the opportunity was lost. By the way, their competitor in this instance was the Product Manager who pleaded for more time and then quit to start his own business capitalising on the opportunity.

This situation taught me a very important rule – UNDERSTAND! Because knowledge is only helpful if you 'have it when you need it' and you can UNDERSTAND how to apply it!

A key lesson in this book is to help you understand what is going on in Your Business and why? Who is controlling what? Who understands how it works? What can be made better, and how can you make that happen?

Challenge: Do you understand how to control your Business?
A:

These challenges will help identify what you already know and what you want to know from SWEAR at Your Business and while you can open any chapter for advice on that topic, your knowledge is made stronger by 'understanding' the information that came in the chapters before. So read on, or jump about, but be happy to go back and learn what you need to know!

By the way, SWEAR at Your Business is an acronym and it stands for - **S**ee **W**eekly **E**xpense & **A**ctivity **R**eports and by the end of this book you will realise why that approach works, why people respond well to it and why it stops situations becoming problems!

As we explore how to apply this to Your Business you may realise that you have heard some of these *lessons* before, some may now make sense for the first time; and others will be new ideas that you will have to think about – which is good because the overall aim is to help you understand situations that you find yourself in and give you the ability to challenge the ideas and the advice that you have to consider for Your Business.

Join me now as we start by turning back the clock to 1899 in what I like to think is best be described as a trip 'back to *your* future'.

About Message to Garcia

Author's note: This is one of the classics of business literature and one of the top ten selling books of the all time (I believe it ranks second).

Not long after starting as a junior exec with an international company I was asked by a director to do something totally out of left field - to find someone who could spray paint the company's typewriters (I'll let the younger readers find out what they are). It didn't occur to me to ask why? I just assumed he had his reasons. After I arranged for someone to paint the models, that were to be used for a new product display, I received a letter from the Director thanking me and adding that it was refreshing to find someone who would 'carry a message to Garcia'.

I had no idea what he was talking about and in those days before the internet I had no easy way to find out. Of course I didn't want to appear stupid by asking him or anyone else what it meant, in case it was something I was supposed to know, so I went to the library to research what 'taking the message to Garcia' was all about. What I read made an immediate impact on me – it described exactly what I had done and what I was even then doing. 'Garcia' and its message of 'accept the challenge and finding a way to tackle the task' became a trait in my approach to business and life.

Over the years I, like many other's have recommend it as an inspiration to team members and as an insight to improving Your Business's productivity. Since it is in the public domain you may legally copy and use the text.

Foreword by Elbert Hubbard (by the Author)

"This literary trifle, A Message to Garcia, was written one evening after supper, in a single hour. It was on the 22nd of February, 1899, Washington's Birthday: we were just going to press with the March Philistine.

The thing leaped hot from my heart, written after a trying day, when I had been endeavouring to train some rather delinquent villagers to abjure the comatose state and get radioactive.

The immediate suggestion, though, came from a little argument over the teacups, when my boy Bert suggested that Rowan was the real hero of the Cuban War. Rowan had gone alone and done the thing - carried the message to Garcia.

It came to me like a flash! Yes, the boy is right; the hero is the man who does his work - who carries the message to Garcia. I got up from the table, and wrote A Message to Garcia. I thought so little of it that we ran it in the Magazine without a heading. The edition went out, and soon orders began to come for extra copies of the March Philistine, a dozen, fifty, a hundred, and when the American News Company ordered a thousand, I asked one of my helpers which article it was that stirred up the cosmic dust. "It's the stuff about Garcia," he said.

The next day a telegram came from George H. Daniels, of the New York Central Railroad thus, "Give price on one hundred thousand Rowan article in pamphlet form - Empire State Express advertisement on back - also how soon can ship."

I replied giving price, and stated we could supply the pamphlets in two years. Our facilities were small and a hundred thousand booklets looked like an awful undertaking. The result was that I gave Mr. Daniels permission to reprint the article in his own way. He issued it in booklet form in editions of half a million. Two or three of these half-million lots were sent out by Mr. Daniels, and in addition the article was reprinted in over two hundred magazines and newspapers. It has been translated into all written languages.

At the time Mr. Daniels was distributing A Message to Garcia, Prince Hilakoff, Director of Russian Railways, was in this country. He was the guest of the New York Central, and made a tour of the country under the personal direction of Mr. Daniels. The Prince saw the little book and was interested in it, more because Mr. Daniels was putting it out in big numbers, probably, than otherwise. In any event, when he got home he had the matter translated into Russian, and a copy of the booklet given to every railroad employee in Russia.

Other countries then took it up, and from Russia it passed into Germany, France, Spain, Turkey, Hindustan and China. During the war between Russia and Japan, every Russian soldier who went to the front was given a copy of A Message to Garcia. The Japanese, finding the booklets in possession of the Russian prisoners, concluded it must be a good thing, and accordingly translated it into Japanese. And on an order of the Mikado, a copy was given to every man in the employ of the Japanese Government, soldier or civilian.

Over forty million copies of A Message to Garcia have been printed. This is said to be a larger circulation than any other literary venture has ever attained during the lifetime of an author, in all history - thanks to a series of lucky accidents."

Elbert Hubbard
December 1913

A Message to Garcia by Elbert Hubbard

In all this Cuban business there is one man stands out on the horizon of my memory like Mars at Perihelion.

When war broke out between Spain and the United States it was very necessary to communicate quickly with the leader of the Insurgents. Garcia was somewhere in the mountain vastness of Cuba - no one knew where. No mail nor telegraph message could reach him. The President must secure his cooperation, and quickly. What to do!

Someone said to the President, "There's a fellow by the name of Rowan will find Garcia for you, if anybody can."

Rowan was sent for and given a letter to be delivered to Garcia. How "the fellow by the name of Rowan" took the letter, sealed it up in an oil-skin pouch, strapped it over his heart, in four days landed by night off the coast of Cuba from an open boat, disappeared into the jungle, and in three weeks came out on the other side of the Island, having traversed a hostile country on foot, and delivered his letter to Garcia – are things I have no special desire now to tell in detail. The point that I wish to make is this: McKinley gave Rowan a letter to be delivered to Garcia; Rowan took the letter and did not ask, "Where is he at?"

By the Eternal! there is a man whose form should be cast in deathless bronze and the statue placed in every college of the land. It is not book-learning young men need, nor instruction about this and that, but a stiffening of the vertebrae which will cause them to be loyal to a trust, to act promptly, concentrate their energies: do the thing - "Carry a message to Garcia!"

General Garcia is dead now, but there are other Garcia's. No man who has endeavored to carry out an enterprise where many hands were needed, but has been well-nigh appalled at times by the imbecility of the average man - the inability or unwillingness to concentrate on a thing and do it.

Slipshod assistance, foolish inattention, dowdy indifference, and half-hearted work seem the rule; and no man succeeds, unless by hook or crook or threat he forces or bribes other men to assist him; or mayhap, God in His goodness performs a miracle, and sends him an Angel of Light for an assistant.

You, reader, put this matter to a test: You are sitting now in your office - six clerks are within call. Summon any one and make this request: "Please look in the encyclopedia and make a brief memorandum for me concerning the life of Correggio." Will the clerk quietly say, "Yes, sir," and go do the task?

On your life, he will not. He will look at you out of a fishy eye and ask one or more of the following questions: Who was he?   Which encyclopedia? Where is the encyclopedia?   Was I hired for that? Don't you mean Bismarck?   What's the matter with Charlie doing it?   Is he dead?   Is there any hurry?   Shan't I bring you the book and let you look it up yourself?   What do you want to know for?

And I will lay you ten to one that after you have answered the questions, and explained how to find the information, and why you want it, the clerk will go off and get one of the other clerks to help him try to find Garcia - and then come back and tell you there is no such man. Of course I may lose my bet, but according to the Law of Average, I will not.

Now, if you are wise, you will not bother to explain to your "assistant" that Correggio is indexed under the C's, not in the K's, but you will smile very sweetly and say, "Never mind," and go look it up yourself. And this incapacity for independent action, this moral stupidity, this infirmity of the will, this unwillingness to cheerfully catch hold and lift -these are the things that put pure Socialism so far into the future. If men will not act for themselves, what will they do when the benefit of their effort is for all?

A first-mate with knotted club seems necessary; and the dread of getting "the bounce" Saturday night holds many a worker to his place. Advertise for a stenographer, and nine out of ten who apply can neither spell nor punctuate - and do not think it necessary to.

Can such a one write a letter to Garcia?

"You see that bookkeeper?" said the foreman to me in a large factory. "Yes! What about him?" "Well he's a fine accountant, but if I'd send him up town on an errand, he might accomplish the errand all right, and on the other hand, might stop at four saloons on the way, and when he got to Main Street would forget what he had been sent for. "Can such a man be entrusted to carry a message to Garcia?

We have recently been hearing much maudlin sympathy expressed for the "downtrodden denizens of the sweat-shop" and "the homeless wanderer searching for honest employment," and with it all often go many hard words for the men in power.

Nothing is said about the employer who grows old before his time in a vain attempt to get frowsy ne'er-do-wells to do intelligent work; and his long, patient striving after "help" that does nothing but loaf when his back is turned.

In every store and factory there is a constant weeding-out process going on. The employer is constantly sending away "help" that have shown their incapacity to further the interests of the business, and others are being taken on. No matter how good times are, this sorting continues: only, if times are hard and work is scarce, the sorting is done finer - but out and forever out the incompetent and unworthy go. It is the survival of the fittest. Self-interest prompts every employer to keep the best - those who can carry a message to Garcia.

I know one man of really brilliant parts who has not the ability to manage a business of his own, and yet who is absolutely worthless to any one else, because he carries with him constantly the insane suspicion that his employer is oppressing, or intending to oppress, him. He cannot give orders; and he will not receive them.

Should a message be given him to take to Garcia, his answer would probably be, "Take it yourself!"

Tonight this man walks the streets looking for work, the wind whistling through his threadbare coat. No one who knows him dare employ him, for he is a regular firebrand of discontent. He is impervious to reason, and the only thing that can impress him is the toe of a thick-soled Number Nine boot.

Of course I know that one so morally deformed is no less to be pitied than a physical cripple; but in our pitying, let us drop a tear, too, for the men who are striving to carry on a great enterprise, whose working hours are not limited by the whistle, and whose hair is fast turning white through the struggle to hold in line dowdy indifference, slipshod imbecility, and the heartless ingratitude which, but for their enterprise, would be both hungry and homeless.

Have I put the matter too strongly? Possibly I have; but when all the world has gone a-slumming I wish to speak a word of sympathy for the man who succeeds - the man who, against great odds, has directed the efforts of others, and having succeeded, finds there's nothing in it: nothing but bare board and clothes. I have carried a dinner pail and worked for day's wages, and I have also been an employer of labor, and I know there is something to be said on both sides.

There is no excellence, per se, in poverty; rags are no recommendation; and all employers are not rapacious and high-handed, any more than all poor men are virtuous. My heart goes out to the man who does his work when the "boss" is away, as well as when he is at home. And the man who, when given a letter for Garcia, quietly takes the missive, without asking any idiotic questions, and with no lurking intention of chucking it into the nearest sewer, or of doing aught else but deliver it, never gets "laid off" nor has to go on a strike for higher wages.

Civilization is one long anxious search for just such individuals. Anything such a man asks shall be granted. He is wanted in every city, town and village - in every office, shop, store and factory. The world cries out for such: he is needed and needed badly - the man who can "Carry a Message to Garcia."

Elbert Hubbard - 1899

1 THE FIRST LESSON IN BUSINESS

> **Challenge:** What makes *you* follow a leader?
> A:

It doesn't matter what problems you are having in business, they can be fixed - it is true when people say "that they've all been had before". 'Message to Garcia' (written in 1896) described problems that businesses faced then ... the same problems that businesses face today!

So it doesn't matter if you run a small business, a corner shop, a multi-national conglomerate or a part of one - the problems are the same (maybe just bigger or smaller), and the answers are the same and they can be found in good-old-fashioned logic. Best of all these are things you can learn and remember; and start benefiting from TODAY!

So let's get started ...

You probably started out with the idea to *'build a better mousetrap so the world would beat a path to your door!'* ... and that worked well until someone built a 'better' better mousetrap and then what happened? Competition! Now you're in business!

Some people say success in business doesn't come easy - it takes hard work! Hard work to get it started, hard work to build it up and hard work to keep it going. Other people will say you can be successful overnight and they'll offer you ideas to follow and examples of success to prove it… Hell, they'll even sell you a franchise! Personally I don't know!

I've met people who have reached success both ways, and it seems largely to depend on the fortunes of timing - having the right product in the right place at the right time. There I go again, talking about things that happen at 'the right time'.

Have you heard the urban legend that says 'An entrepreneur must fail seven times before they can succeed'? True, according to many entrepreneurs; but maybe it's just that when they the hit market for the seventh time they hit it at the RIGHT time?

So is success (instant or otherwise) more a case of hard work, good timing or just plain old good luck?

Let's digress for a minute and consider Fred; he's a wannabe property investor who buys a house to rent out, the property market jumps up and he has to decide to keep renting it or to sell the property?

Now, whether he makes the right decision or not and whether he makes a profit or a loss is not important to us (we can explore Fred's real estate world another day); what is important to us is that Fred was there! He was in the marketplace, at the right time to take advantage of that opportunity when it came his way.

Success in business comes down to being there for when opportunity arrives; and whether it comes for you, sooner or later depends on YOUR timing – when you get into the market, what you do to promote your idea and what you do to keep your business afloat. But know this, when your time comes (and even outdated products and ideas have a habit of recycling back into fashion) being there and being ready to respond will make the difference between seizing the opportunity or not – that is the difference between success or failure.

Your business will probably go through many stages – getting the doors open ... your first sale ... the struggle ...surviving the first year ... more struggle ... growth ... some comfort (?) ... ups and downs ... then (hopefully) ... market domination.

And to achieve any of these milestones and to be there for when your opportunity arrives, you must first do ONE thing. "What is that you ask?"

The number one lesson for succeeding in business is 'DO NOT FAIL'.

SWEAR at Your Business

"Of course none of us imagine failure as being an option, until it arrives – after all how could our great idea not set the world on fire … or how could the success we've had locally not multiply across the country and around the world … how could anyone not want our fantastic product or service?

You know, I have never seen 'Failure' listed as one of the options in a business plan or included as part of an investment strategy presented to a bank manager. No, we do not give failure, or ways to avoid it enough thought … until it arrives.

So what do you think, is <u>now</u> a good time to start making sure Your Business will 'NOT FAIL'?

Let's start by simplifying Your Business – understanding how all the parts work and interact with each other – and along the way finding out what can go wrong and how to stop it!

2 SIMPLIFYING BUSINESS

Challenge: What does Your Business do?
A:

For many people the business entity is a complex and scary thing – it must be because people study for years to learn how to manage them, right?

Then again, many of them get it wrong and their businesses don't survive – so what did they know; all this while the local tradesman or shop owner just goes on making profit and being successful ... in their own quiet way.

Perhaps Your Business needs to be less complex?

Of course it was once less complex, back when it started, probably just the owner and one or two staff – everyone doing their part and knowing what everyone else was doing as well. But as the business grew it became less simple - it needed more parts, more people, more structure etc.

So, let's look at how we can simplify your business (again); by breaking it back down into small easy to understand parts.

The business you work for may seem to be a very complex entity - it may have branches everywhere, a vast range of products and a multitude of clients; and all demand different handling to meet their different expectations;

But if we simplify what the business does, we'll find that the business or department, infact Your Business is made up of just ...

Four *FUNCTIONS* (*things that it does*) -
    DEMAND
    SUPPLY
    PRODUCTION
    CONTROL

Four *FACTORS* (*things that will affect it*) -
    STAFF
    REPUTATION
    CULTURE
    MARKETPLACE

And three *RULES* (*that will influence results*) -
    Rule 1: KISS
    Rule 2: UNDERSTAND
    Rule 3: PAL

OK, the first thing you are doing is thinking through this list to see what's missing, to see if it fits Your Business, or not?

That's good, questioning, rather than just accepting the information – so let's make it a challenge.

> **Challenge:** *Can you find any aspect of your business that does not fit into the 'functions' listed below –*
>
> - *DEMAND – sales, marketing, advertising, PR*
> - *SUPPLY – delivery: goods in & out*
> - *PRODUCTION – manufacture / service / warehouse*
> - *CONTROL – supervision, administration*
>
> A:

If something didn't seem to fit that's ok, write it down; we'll look at that a bit later but I'll bet this still makes your business seem far less complex than you previously thought it was?

And, if you've never thought of your business in such simple terms before, then it's time to do so. Because keeping it simple is what this is going to be all about.

Which brings us to the first of the three golden rules will help Your Business success.

3 RULE # 1 - KISS

> **Challenge:** How much time do you spend solving problems?
> A:

As advice rules go, this is an oldie, but a goody! Sometimes you see it written in different ways –

- **Keep it simple, stupid!** Don't make it harder than you have to.

- **Keep it stupid simple!** So anybody can understand it.

However you say it KISS means do not to over-complicate things that we have to do, like –
- Make decisions
- Planning activities
- Give directions

In each decision you must make - consider the easiest answers first. For example, a motor mechanic I know once spent all day dismantling and rebuilding the differential in a car, only to find out that the 'growling' sound was actually caused by the exhaust pipe rubbing on the bodywork. The sound was the same as a faulty crown wheel makes when the car cornered to the right – good diagnosis of the problem BUT because he didn't work from the simplest to the hardest possible option he didn't find the true cause until later in the day and on that job he lost both time and money … and by telling us, his friends, he lost a bit of his reputation as well.

Try listing all the options (or at least 3 ways to do it) in ascending order (easiest to do to hardest) and then work through them, one by one. You may still find that the answer was the last on the list, but in all probability the easier causes will have been quicker to diagnose and the problem, if one of them, will have been easier to solve.

Don't complicate your life, if you cannot control the problem or influence its outcome don't waste your time looking for the answer, instead look at how to lessen its impact on Your Business. When GST was introduced in Australia, many businessmen spent hours stressing about how to get around it, rather than how to absorb it into their business model and get on with life. They made a major source of concern out of something they couldn't control anyway. KISS means – simplify the problem and spend your time on things you can change, not those you cannot.

Of course you have to consider each problem as it arises, but the key is to decide how much time should be spent on it and by whom?
- Is it a problem or a process issue?
- Whose problem or issue?
- Can it be resolved or should you risk assess it and plan damage-control?
- What will it affect, what damage can it do?
- Must YOU solve it or can you delegate it?

To understand how this works – ask yourself the following questions about the last problem you spent time on?
- Did you resolve it, or was it out of your control?
- Did you think from the simplest to hardest option?
- Could you have delegated it to someone?
- How long did it take to reach a conclusion?
- How much time was wasted?

Keeping it simple stupid saves you time and money by eliminate waste - not spending time and resources (yours and others) in the wrong way.

Make sure anyone can understand it. We have all had the experience of not knowing what someone was talking about and maybe having to ask them or others to explain it to us.

For example, in business have you ever been given an instruction that was so long-winded, vague or complicated that you needed a road map to follow the job? How did the job go? Was it completed on time, on budget and stress-free? Probably not!

Have you ever given instructions like that? How many times did it take <u>them</u> to get it right? How was your stress level? How was theirs?

Keeping it stupid simple eliminates, or at least reduces, the chance of mistakes being made as a result of miscommunication or misunderstanding.

This makes it sound like KISS is two separate rules but it is not - by applying KISS to all your thinking (decisions, directions and problems) you will improve productivity and job satisfaction for yourself, your team and Your Business.

Applying KISS -
- Think simple!
- Look for the easiest way to do things.
- Don't over complicate your planning.
- Don't overcomplicate your explanations to others.
- Problem solving – work from the easiest to hardest possible answer.

4 RULE # 2 - UNDERSTAND

Challenge: Do you know every role in Your Business?
A:

Rule number two means what it says: Understand.

This means - <u>understand your business</u>, what your business is, what it can do, how it does it, what your client's want and how you can deliver that, efficiently.

This is a most important rule, and to emphasise its importance I want to relate it back to an earlier statement - before a business can succeed it must first NOT FAIL

But businesses do fail all the time, some are small and go unnoticed (except by the owner and the employees of course, who lose everything); however some are large, even spectacular and these receive public attention with the media speculating how and why they imploded.

You don't need to look behind the scenes for the reasons they failed, the headlines will tell the story - the boss didn't know, the facts weren't clear, by the time we knew it was too late, someone took their eye off the ball, blah, blah!

Large or small, ALL businesses fail for the same reason (except for cases of outright fraud and theft) **businesses fail because they didn't understand their business**. The boss didn't know what was or wasn't going on and the company 'methodology' lacked the processes to tell him in time.

Let me say that again - **the boss didn't know what was going on and the company systems couldn't tell him in time!**

Recently, governments have been calling for; and business gurus have been espousing the need for better 'corporate governance' which in simple language means - the boss knowing what's going on in the business… in time to fix problems!

Unfortunately 'I don't know' and 'I forgot' have become common excuses that have found their way into, and affected many businesses, maybe even yours.

But this can be avoided or changed by making UNDERSTANDING not just a responsibility (which it is supposed to be anyway) but a part of the philosophy that drives every person and monitors every level of Your Business, at all times.

As a business leader understanding what you need to know is not the same as understanding what should go on ... and what does!

> **Challenge:** Ask yourself –
> - Do you know what everyone in your business does?
> - How they do it?
> - And why they do it that way?
> - If not, do you know who DOES know?
> - Do your Team Leaders know what their people do; how they do it and why?
> - Does the business system know (& report) that every step of every process is correct?
> - Can you check on the performance of any one step at any time ... easily?
>
> A:

If you answered NO to any of the above questions it may mean that your business is lacking in 'good corporate governance'.

Of course it might not; but the point is you don't know, because you don't UNDERSTAND all of the functions of the business. So now is the time to correct that. Ask the above questions about every part of Your Business until YOU are certain that the answer is "YES I UNDERSTAND!"

I cannot stress enough the importance to success of understanding - it is a recurring theme in much of what you will read shortly; and it should become a habit of yours ... to understand Your Business.

Applying UNDERSTAND –

Everyone should -
Understand how Your Business works.
Understand *their* part in the business.
Understand how it works with others.
Understand the likely consequences of every action before starting it.
Understand the outcome wanted/ expected from a decision, before making it.

Decision makers should always ask questions - who, what, why, when, where and how?
- Who does what in Your Business?
- How they do it?
- Why they do it ... that way?
- Why did it happen?

When you want to know something - keep asking 'why' until you understand why!

This is Toyota's secret to achieving great quality control - when something goes wrong they ask WHY at each step, working back through the process, until they find the actual cause? Then they can understand it and they fix it so it won't happen again.

Understand how to solve problems by considering at least three options - find 3 different ways to do the task ... and challenge each of the three - I guarantee during this process you will *understand* which one is the best option to use, and why!

Understanding people problems will be covered in detail elsewhere in this book and in SWEAR at Your Staff, but using the above technique - asking questions – will allow you to *understand* that it is a people problem.

One more thought on the benefit of understanding. Have you ever had to address a problem or issue that was the same as one you had handled before? I'll bet it worked out well because you understood the situation, the problem and the best way to handle it. Most people don't make mistakes when they UNDERSTAND!

5 RULE # 3 - PAL

> **Challenge:** How much time do you spend solving problems?
> A:

Rule number three: Profit = Assets - Liabilities.

We have all heard the saying 'everything in life that you do or have, is either good or bad for you' and in business terms this means, that everything is either an asset (good) or a liability (bad) for you.

We also understand that everything has an up and a down side, and often we have to find and accept the balance.

For example, if you play golf (or any sport) on the weekend; what do you put off doing to make available that time? If you own a boat, jet ski or similar toy; how much more does it cost you to own and use per hour; what else could you do with that money? Do you have a worker who you think is a not pulling his/ her weight; how long will you carry them?

These everyday choices show that you understand the concept of PAL - you already make allowances for things that cost you time and money - but have you stopped to think about how much these choices cost you? It is now time to think of them as assets and liabilities.

This doesn't mean that you have to stop playing golf or get rid of the toys; it means that you have to understand the consequences of the choices that you make, to get the balance right.

Profit equals Assets less Liabilities

Not just in the balance sheet but in every part of your business - everything, every purchase and every person will be either an asset or a liability; and to make a profit you MUST HAVE more assets than liabilities.

To understand this you must examine each function of your business to determine if it is an asset or a liability. If you are not sure how to assess it, or how to make it into an asset, then you probably don't understand that function well enough ... so go back to Rule 2.

Some things are easier to measure than others, for example - would you buy a $1 million machine for a one off job, or would you rent it?

But others are not so easy to measure; and it all boils down to what's in it for the business:
1. Is every job profitable?
2. Does every department work efficiently?
3. Are all Managers and Supervisors fully utilized and cost covered?
4. Do you consider waste as a form of liability (because it does cost you money)?
5. Does Your Business identify how and where waste can be reduced?
6. Does each person's workload match the hours they work?
7. Do jobs 'spread out' to fill the available time?
8. Do you even know?

PAL affects every aspect of your business and the process of converting liabilities into assets may take time, but it is not hard and it is worth it for the increase to your profits!

Assessing functions as an asset or a liability
starts with –
- Understanding what result you want each function of Your Business to achieve.
- Measuring the results it is achieving.
- Deciding if it is performing the best (most effective) way possible.
- Identifying what changes may improve the performance.
- Being prepared to release (dispose of) anything that cannot be made into an asset.

Implementing changes within the functions that are necessary to convert it into an asset may require you to get people to 'embrace' and 'take ownership' of new ideas and methods, and we will look at doing this in later chapters.

Making changes stick is another matter altogether and this is something that will require either constant vigilance on your part OR a change in the company methodology (the way things are done) to enable these changes to become part of the daily process so that they stay in place and work the way that you want them to. It is also important to recognise the impact that these changes will have on the various factors* of your business

Applying PAL -
- Everything in your business will be either an asset or a liability.
- Every person in your business will be either an asset or a liability.
- Identify and keep your assets and correct or change or replace your liabilities.
- To make a profit you need to have more assets than liabilities!

*Factors are things that influence your business and their impact depends on if they are a positive or negative force - we need to examine these as being liabilities and change them into assets.

6 STAFF
(Your # 1 liability in business)

> **Challenge:** What did you enjoying about being an employee?
> A:

Employees are the number one liability of Your Business!

"What you say? Management books say that employees are my business' # 1 asset".

And they should be, and they can be … if they are regularly serviced and maintained, just like all the other assets in your business. For example - how long does a truck remain an asset without regular maintenance? Breakdowns, lost income, frustration etc would soon see it being repaired or moved on and replaced.

Employees are the same, in fact some employers may advocate 'either they work or they go' and while this is not the message here it is a reality of business economics and has been since the start of time (ie; people have to perform to keep their job).

Manpower management trends suggest moving the company emphasis from such areas as customer service to what is now seen as the more important area of ... employee satisfaction ... the theory being that a happy worker is a good worker!

It doesn't need to be this dramatic, it shouldn't be about service OR staff – it should be about offering people a fair deal and a chance to feel good about what they're getting – I know this sounds like the deal that we're offering the customer <u>and</u> it is – it's also the same deal we should be offering to our staff.

Understanding Employees
Employees are people like you (and me) and like us they respond to certain motivators; almost without exception we all have two basic needs from our job –

1. We need to understand where we FIT – what we are meant to do and why?

2. We need to know that we are APPRECIATED – that what we do, matters!

Of course these two principles alone WILL NOT replace a good wages, bonuses and benefits program, but we all perform better with a pat on the back and when we know why we are doing what it is that we have to do.

When you started in business you probably needed a few good workers and you went out of your way to make sure they knew that they were appreciated; but as the business grows we sometimes forget this and we don't make each one feel as important as we once did ... Why?

The two most common causes of staff friction, and resignations, are the belief that either 'I do more than he does' and / or 'I'm not appreciated'.

> **Challenge:** Think back to some of your earlier jobs –
> - Which didn't you like and why did you quit?
> - What was your favourite job – why did you like it?
>
> A:

It's a fair bet that **fitting in** and **being appreciated** had an impact on those decisions AND what's more they are <u>still</u> in your memory ... even now! That's how powerful a motivator, or turn-off, they can be.

So imagine if you had a business where each employee knew what was expected of them, and of their co-workers; how their efforts fitted into the overall business model, leaving no room for friction, confusion or employee discontent. Wouldn't you want to work in place like that?

Having staff **understand** the impact that they make in the business, as well as feeling that they are part of the business process will create a more enthusiastic workforce – staff will become team members who are loyal, eager and keen to respond to the needs of your clients and the challenges of your marketplace!

If you're still not convinced of the importance staff management has; or it sounds too simple to be the answer? Then let's explore a few examples -

Example 1 - Does your business have a 'Suggestion Box'? It's a popular practice that companies try (from time to time) to encourage employees to be involved and offer suggestions on ways that might improve the business; but what happens next? –

Company A gives the suggestion to the immediate supervisor to assess because he knows how his department works; and then management is surprised when he rejects the idea because it either doesn't mesh with the needs of other workers or because it diminishes his control (not that he says that), either way the idea is rejected, management forget it and the employee doesn't bother offering any further suggestions.

Company B has an 'open understanding' philosophy, where each employee knows how their work interacts in the business and with those around them, including supervisors and controls etc; so any idea placed in that suggestion box will be a more complete picture of how the idea will fit in, what changes may be needed and what benefits it will deliver. In fact, in this environment more people may have provided input to the idea and so management and the supervisor can see more accurately how it will impact and be able to judge the idea on its merit.

Wouldn't you rather be managing Company B?

Example 2 - If you employ salespeople, are they encouraged to look beyond your existing client base to find new business opportunities? Of course they are! You want them to understand where the business has come from and where it is going; to know about new clients you are chasing – you may even have them compare notes about potential clients that they may have dealt with before. You tell your sales team about each new deal and each new client that the business gets – to motivate them to seek more of the same.

But do you tell the factory staff? Wouldn't it motivate them as well? Wouldn't they like to hear about how the business is growing? And it may be that they know someone there or have an idea that will help to keep a problem client. They may even have dealt with that potential new client at another job and can show you ways to improve the relationship.

Sharing news about the business with ALL team members is a great way ensures they feel involved – do this and they will celebrate the wins and be looking for ways to help get more of them!

Example 3 - Have you ever had to defend a staff wrongful dismissal or a discrimination or harassment charge? If you cringed at the mere thought of it; that's ok because these types of claims have been known to put a shiver down the back of many a tough businessmen.

Why? Because they know, from bitter experience, that to get to this stage the matter has been badly handled by a company officer (or it wouldn't be an problem). Plus, they know the time it will take to fight it and the cost in penalties it may incur, not to mention the possibility of having to rehire a now troublesome employee.

Wouldn't it have been easier if in the beginning your Supervisor knew exactly how to handle this matter and prevent it from becoming a problem?

Example 4 – It's 3am, you're sound asleep and the phone rings, you swear under your breath, apologise to the wife for waking her up, and then what do you say to the Supervisor who rang you asking for advice on a problem? You tell him that it's ok that he rang, and then you answer his question.

How much easier would it be for everyone (especially the wife) if the Supervisor knew where to get that answer in the first place, without having to disturb you?

All these examples advocate sharing knowledge in your business, about developing an 'open understanding' philosophy that allows everyone access to 'know-how' when they need it, at any time?

Understanding comes from two sources – experience and / or instruction.
- Experience - having done something before and learning from the outcomes.
- Instruction - having access to guidance in how to do something, based on other people's previous experience.

Understanding your staff can turn your biggest (potential) liability into an asset - by creating an environment where your employees understand their part in and benefit to Your Business.

There is also a more tangible benefit that comes from having happy, motivated employees. How much of your wages bill is spent on staff costs. like supervision and recruitment / replacement? If having 'open understanding' could cut staff turnover (and recruiting costs) by 20% and new staff training and supervision costs by 25% then how much time and money will that save? That extra money is profit for your business!

And if you're still not sure how important the Staff factor is to Your Business, then consider this –

***STAFF** will affect & influence every **FUNCTION** of your business – demand, supply, production and control!*

7 Your Business Reputation
(Your # 2 liability in business)

> **Challenge:** What did others think about Your Business?
> A:

Reputation is defined as being '*what is generally said or believed about the character of a person or thing*'.

So what is generally said or believed about the character or reputation of Your Business?

And how do you know?

Most people believe, rightly so, that a reputation must be earned. So is your business earning a good reputation or do you just take it for granted (and hope) that enough customers and people like you?

Does your favourite client think your business is -
        a) Of good character?
        b) Just good enough to do a reasonable job?
        c) The best of a bad lot?
        d) A contractual obligation?

What about that sale you didn't get or the customer you just lost, how much do you think reputation affected their decision not to deal with you?

The success of Your Business relies on having a good reputation and so it is important that you understand this factor; and how to turn it from a liability into an asset.

The simplest way to understand about your reputation is to ask those that know!

Find out what your clients think of you -
- Ask your customers what they think you do well and what you do not so well?
- Ask the same question of customers you have just lost or failed to win?
- Understand what they say; and what they mean; and what they want you to change.
- Examine how much of this you can adapt into your business (but remember you cannot be all things to all people).

Now that you understand what your business' reputation is, you can either accept it or set out to 'earn' a new, better one.

This may involve changes to some of your business methods (such as are those being suggested in this book) that may take time to adopt. Certainly it will be of interest to those who work for and interact with Your Business

Involve your staff in the assessment and change process from the beginning – let them contribute to (and have ownership of) the process and the outcomes – after all they are the ones that will have to make it work and they are the ones who will sell the benefits (or not) to your customers.

Involve clients in these changes process by selling the changes you are making and showing how they, the customer, will benefit from the changes (this may help keep a client from leaving) especially if the idea is something they suggested.

Involve ex-clients in these changes process by explaining the changes being made and showing how the new dynamic business approach can benefit and assist them (it might win back some old customers).

And remember, while these changes may take time to fully implement, they will help improve service to your existing customers and attract new ones along the way and that means your business reputation is now changing from a liability to becoming an asset.

8 COMPANY CULTURE
(A factor & liability # 3)

> **Challenge:** What did employees think about Your Business?
> A:

Good company culture is vital to your business because it determines 'how we do things around here' – it is the environment that affects how your staff feel about working in Your Business - and the attitude they will reflect it in dealings with each other and with your customers!

Before we can understand if Company Culture is an asset or a liability, infact before we understand how culture works, we need to understand what culture IS.

The dictionary defined culture as -
1) **How we behave!** A particular form of manners.
2) **How we treat other people!** The philosophy that governs behaviour and courtesy between people in a (civilisation or) workplace.

So culture in Your Business is how we behave and how we treat others; and as a result, how everyone gets along and the *feeling* they have about being here!

If we want to create a good company culture then ideally it would be one that makes everyone *feel* good about working here and motivates and inspires them to try that little bit harder.

An atmosphere that makes them feel a part of the team… where they are stakeholders* with a vested interest in the success of the business.

*Stakeholders are those who stand to gain from the business' success or lose from its failure. Traditionally, stakeholders were considered to be the business founder/ entrepreneur and the shareholders (who in a failure might lose their investments); while in more recent times business has began to woo clients to think of themselves as being stakeholders in the business, in an effort to tie in their loyalty (they may lose their price or market advantage).

Isn't it time we made the same offer to our staff?

In fact, those with the most to gain or lose in the business are you and your staff (you all lose jobs, income, family security, lifestyle etc) and because you both work in the business and need it to be successful you both have a shared responsibility for creating the best, most suitable, success-driven environment or culture that you can.

Do your staff members see themselves as being stakeholders with a vested interest in the business' success? Do they see their long term future with this business? Do they enjoy being here? Why do they come to work here each day?

> **Challenge:** Find out how your employees view their work experience – ask them to assist in a 'looking for new ideas' exercise (without repercussions and the only promise being to look at what might be possible). Ask each person to nominate -
> - 2 things that they like about their job.
> - 2 things they would change if they could.
>
> A:

If you need to create a better culture in your business then a good place to start is by understanding what your staff want and trying to develop a business model that strives to motivate them by offering it. This will have a positive impact on current employees and set the expectations for the future – new employees want to come to work in a positive, exciting, successful, stress free and fun workplace.

9 THE MARKETPLACE
(The factor that's beyond your control)

> **Challenge:** How do you compare to your main competitors?
> A:

The marketplace is the one factor that is beyond your control!

In spite of what your ego may think, you cannot control *everything* around you; a fact expressed by John Lennon who wrote *'life is what happens while you're busy making other plans'* ... AND for those of us who have learned this lesson the hard way there is another useful quote that sums up that feeling you have after the dust has settled, this one from Ned Kelly ... *'Such is life'*.

We want to be pro-active and avoid those 'such is life' moments but how many times have you made plans that didn't work out because someone or something changed the rules in the marketplace?

The marketplace is where you and others do business; and while you are busy making your plans others are busy making theirs and because neither of you compare notes you can bet that some of their plans will affect Your Business. For example a competitor may launch a new product and grab a share of your market; or a client may (not having read this advice) go broke, costing you market share and money. You must realise that disasters like these (and others) do happen to businesses somewhere every day, you usually can't see it coming ... and you can't stop it from happening when it does.

"Great news!" you say "so how am I meant to avoid a disaster I can't see coming?"

And the answer is YOU CAN'T!

You can't avoid it BUT you can alter how it will affect your business, by HAVING A BACK UP PLAN for how you will live with or without the many things you cannot control, if they happen. For example, you cannot control the weather but if it affects your business you allow for it in quotes and costs and you plan alternate activities for the staff being affected on bad weather days.

This is part of your Strategic Risk Management Register and should include how you plan to counteract unseen and uncontrollable events like -
- Customer changes product requirements
- Customer (say your # 1) collapses due to unforeseen circumstances

- Competitor launches a new product or presentation / sales edge
- Price drop caused by a competitor, government or overseas force.
- Interest rates or raw material prices sky-rocket
- Factory & office burns down (some or everything is lost)
- Key employee's sudden departure to - a) join your competitor, b) leave the industry or c) write a 'tell all' book about your business.
- Staff threatening to go on strike (how will you avoid it or live through it?)
- Spouse files for divorce (and wants half the business)
- Accountant absconds with your savings and / or the operating cash.

The questions you need to ask yourself about each of these (and other) possibilities are -
- What is the impact on your business today, tomorrow and beyond?
- What precautions (plan A) can you put in place to cover such events?
- What alternative options (plan B) can you employ, if all else fails?

Once you have thought this through and are satisfied that you have plan A and an optional plan B & maybe a plan C to fall back on, the best thing you can do is file these ideas away (reviewing them from time to time) and then forget about it (until it happens). Get on with your life because the marketplace is the one element that is truly beyond all of our control.

Of course you must be vigilant to changes in the marketplace but for most people in small business (ie; those without spies) these changes will be seen only after the event. One way you may be able to gain an early warning advantage is to remember Cause and Effect. If you lose a sale or a client this is the effect of something that caused it – identify the cause and analyse it – it may alert you to a more significant problem coming.

By the way if it makes you feel better even Microsoft, inspite of its world domination, has had problems (to which it had to react) caused by other forces in its marketplace.

10 MANAGING LIABILITIES - Part 1
(People are a pain in the butt!)

> **Challenge:** Are there people working for you that you don't like?
> A:

Ok, now you understand the liabilities of Your Business and that it is a good idea to turn them into assets, it may be time to look more closely at how to do this by managing the liabilities.

Naturally, we should start with number one – Staff

We know that we need staff and we need them to be happy and inspite of what good things we try to do for them some people are just a pain in the butt!

In SWEAR at Your Staff we look at this issue in more detail, including why *you* may sometimes be a pain in the butt! Its true, some people may think of you that way at times.

Here we want to focus on how and why people respond the way they do and how that affects Your Business.

We all have our strengths & weaknesses.

It is important in business to understand that people are driven by what motivates and exhilarates them (strengths) and they stall or back off at things that bore or scare them (weaknesses).

Everyone's strengths and weaknesses are different, which is why if you present a problem to a group of people, some can clearly see the solution while others cannot.

Use other people's strengths and weaknesses as a positive way of engaging them in the decision making process – this will give them a better understanding and ownership of the outcome. If using a group to work through a problem present it to the team/ group, as either –
- A) An opportunity for the team members to learn more about this subject.
OR
- B) As a problem so important that it requires some group input or discussion.

You must also understand that a person's strengths and weaknesses will influence decisions they make; which is why, even though the answer appears clear and logical to you, they don't see it.

And you should expect that they will only change their mind once they have a better understanding or a different perspective of the problem.

Which means you may need to re-present the issues in a different scenario to assist this person in seeing the matter in a different (your) perspective.

In case you haven't noticed it, your own strengths and weaknesses work the same way – affecting your ability to clearly see ideas presented by others. To avoid being seen as the 'one who doesn't get it' ask to be given alternative scenarios that better demonstrate how the idea works!

Understanding Personality Conflicts

Sometimes it seems that some people don't want to listen to each other, or they just don't want to get along together - but the problem is slightly more complex than that.

The fact is our response/ reaction to any topic, question or situation will be governed by two things - logic (our understanding of the matter) and emotions (a reaction caused by elements of our own personality).

Emotions vary from day-to-day; and in order to know how and when they will affect reactions, we have to understand how these two elements work.

Understanding of a problem or suggestion will be influenced by our –
- Knowledge of the subject (is it a strength or weakness)
- Comprehension of the presentation being made (our attentiveness)
- Perspective of the situation (how it will impact on us); however ...

Reaction/ response to the situation will often be the result of our emotions (personality traits and moods) which determine 'how we feel at the time'. For example our response to the same request on different days might well vary, if influenced by -
- Our feelings toward the person making the suggestion.
- Our feelings toward the job or situation or the company generally, on the day.
- Timing; if the request were made just after we had received bad personal news.

So, as reaction/ response is the result of the emotions in place at the time – **mood** (how we feel today) and **personality** (how we feel generally) - then recognising these mood and personality traits in others may help in getting a positive outcome or keep control of a situation.

So what are the elements that drive emotions?

Mood swings are a spontaneous reaction to any subject that has a strong emotional meaning for the person and they can be 'triggered' by a reminder or a reference to the topic or just something that causes a memory flash (having a vague thought).

We cannot control mood swings in ourselves or prevent them in others because there are many things that can cause or trigger them, often without us knowing we've done it.

- *The guy in the pub who asks you to stop bragging about your team winning is an understandable reaction to his feelings (bad mood) about his own team losing.*

- *How a smell, a favourite food or a reference to a place that has some (distant connection) to a sad or happy event in your lives can cause a change in our mood.*

Just as these things affect you they work the same way on other people and when you notice a mood change, unless you know what triggered the mood swing, your best response is to –
- Apologise for having upset the person.
- Move on to another subject.
- Defer the matter to a (more receptive) time.

Personality Traits on the other hand, are in-built mechanisms that cause us to respond in a certain way to the same situation every time - they can be identified and understood.

All the personalities in the world fall into one of seven categories – they all have a name and specific traits, which we can look at later – but what we need to know here is how they interact, how each will get along with some and dislike or even clash with others.

If we put 7 people of different personalities in a circle, based on their interaction traits – we would find that they will like those closest to them and dislike those moving further away, this is a natural response known as **The Circle of Friends** –

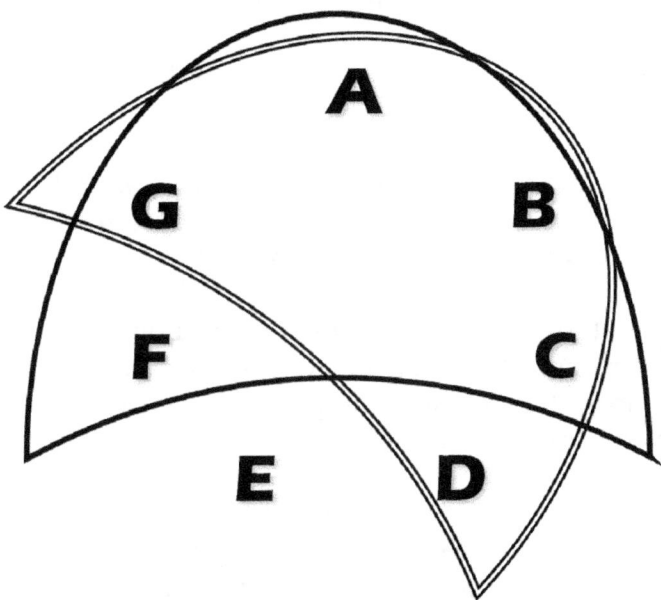

Let's look at what has happened in our circle of friends A – G:

Person A (circle shown in solid black line) -
    Likes B & G
    Thinks C & F are ok
    Dislikes D & E

Person B (circle shown in double line) -
    Likes A & C
    Thinks D & G are ok
    Dislikes E & F.

Here's the problem with personalities!
A likes (and is mates with) B and G.
A and B both agree they dislike E, but A also dislikes D and can't understand why B thinks D is ok; and they also disagree on F (whom A thinks is ok and B dislikes).

Also, because B is mates with C (and A just thinks is ok) it is possible that one day B may be forced to choose between the friendship of A and C.

And don't forget A also has this problem around the other side of the circle with G, F and E; and just to make things worse, this problem starts again for every person in the circle.

This explains why we like some people and not others - we like the personalities nearest to us in this circle; and we are hum-ho about those a step away and dislike those personalities opposite us in the Circle of Friends.

This explains a few things about understanding people –

1. Why we can walk into room and like or dislike someone on sight, even if we've never met them before.

2. Why our friends may like (or accept) someone whom we personally dislike.

3. Why some people have 'personality clashes' with others. If you force an A and a D to work together – there is going to be friction.

4. Why we find it impossible to get along with everybody, even if we try; potentially 2 in every 6 people we meet (ie 1 in every 3) we'll have strong feelings against

Personality is something we cannot alter - we can try to NOT SHOW how we feel but we cannot CHANGE how we feel. And it's very likely that socially you already understand how to manage these situations.

Do you have a brother or sister?

Did you fight with them when you were kids?

As you got older what did you do? You distanced yourself from them or from those subjects that caused conflict. Siblings will tell you that, even as they get older, most can only tolerate each other for short times; and certainly not at all on some subjects. This is what makes family Xmas so frustrating for parents who don't understand the concept of the Circle of Friends.

In business we have to be more tolerant!

You cannot distance yourself from those you work with, you can't just get up and leave the boardroom table or swear at a colleague or tell a client their idea is stupid (well you can but it is not recommended as a positive career move). We have to understand how to handle these things differently because statistically we may have a 'personality conflict' with 33% of the people we meet - and that includes staff, subordinates, clients and the boss!

So how to survive personality conflicts at work?

Understanding the problem is one thing, applying it is another; here are a few suggestions that may help you look at the causes and how they will play out in the workplace -

The BOSS:
Understand that it goes both ways; s/he has personality issues with you as well. Acknowledge

(to yourself) why you cannot agree & accept those different ideas. It may not be practical to discuss this relationship situation with the boss so if you're challenging, what you consider, their poor business advice - do it cautiously and keep the interaction strictly project/ job related.

CLIENTS:
You probably cannot discuss this situation with the client, but do discuss this situation with others in your organisation and, if possible, try to share your responsibility for the client – this way personality clashes can be diffused (by the other) & won't cause the client to want to sack you or your firm. Keep conversations upbeat and project / performance related and follow up all meetings with a written (or email) summary of the points raised or actions discussed (this helps reinforce the work rather than personal feelings at meetings).

EMPLOYEES:
If you employ staff only from the ones you like, you will be cutting the available supply pool down by a third (33%). Base recruiting criteria on job performance requirements; if they turn out to like you, consider it a bonus; and remember you don't have to take your employee home, just work with them, so if s/he is the best person for the job, employ them!

ASSISTANT 2IC:

This is also true when selecting a 2IC – it is hard to select someone whom you do not like but if s/he is right for the position and YOU can find a way to work with them you will end up with a more rounded management team (their opinions of others will differ from yours); they will probably not say 'yes sir' to your suggestions, preferring instead to challenging ideas with alternatives (this is healthy).

Discuss this concept with Keymen.
It is a good idea to discuss the 'Circle of Friends' concept with the Keymen in Your Business – make sure they realise it is a two-way situation, so that everyone understands how this dynamic applies to them and the team they work with.

Motivating & Disciplining
These are two things that, when not done properly, often backfire on Your Business – causing friction between staff. In SWEAR at Your Staff we discuss in detail the concept that the need for both of these comes from staff who fail to meet expectations of performance (motivation) or conduct (discipline); and that either of these is the result of the person being one of three things - disinterested, disillusioned or distracted.

The key purpose in any 1-on-1 meeting with staff should be to find which of these three is causing the problem.

Note: Equipment is Not a Liability

For those who work in engineering or equipment focused businesses who are concerned that I have not included Plant & Equipment in the list of liabilities. This is because Plant & Equipment are not a 'factor' in the business; sure they are an asset, and they can be a headache and an expense and consume a lot of time; but they are not a liability that affects Your Business in their own right.

Let me explain – if you have a machine and you could set it in motion it would do its job exactly as you have programmed it, all day every day; and it will keep doing it for as long as you maintain it and operate it as per the manufacturer's instructions.

Now, what is the factor that affects the ability of this machine to keep functioning properly … to do what it does?

Staff!

The operator who operates it incorrectly, or the serviceman who maintains it poorly or does not check it as they should and/ or replace parts at the optimum time - they are the FACTOR that affects equipment – staff is the liability here!

11 MANAGING LIABILITIES - Part 2
(Safety, risks and obligations of staff)

> **Challenge:** What could do the most harm to Your Business?
> A:

As well as managing the problems (see above) that staff may create, Your Business has an obligation to protect them from themselves and the activities of others - by providing staff with a safe workplace free from -
- **Discrimination**
- **Harassment**
- **Bullying**
- **Wrongful Dismissal**
- **Industrial Relations rights infringements**
- **Health & Safety risks and hazards**

Ask any business owner or manager what they think of having to defend themselves in any of the above? And the unlucky ones (those found guilty) will tell you that the cost is real and it hurts!

SWEAR at Your Business

The obligations of employing staff include many responsibilities set down by law and these have penalties* if you fail to comply. Penalties that can be, and usually are, imposed on the company, its directors, the managers and the supervisor/s who were involved in the incident and / or failed to prevent it from occurring.

* Penalties are usually a monetary fine and or a compensation payout for the victim/s (amounts vary, but can run into thousands of dollars) and in severe cases (resulting in injury or death) the court may include criminal charges and the penalty, in these cases, may include jail time.

"She'll be right Mate!" is not good enough and "I didn't know about that" (with or without a smile) will not excuse you from liability in these matters.

The only acceptable defence that you can rely on (during an investigation or in court) for any of these matters is –
1. The ability to prove that the Company's systems were applied; and ...
2. That they are correct (by law) to monitor and control the situation; and ...
3. That all actions taken by people (like you) were approved (by the system); ...
4. That the outcomes were documented and recorded.

The next few pages looks at each of the 'dangers' to Your Business; and provides the definition and a list of some of the usual traps that people fall into and be advised - <u>each must be avoided at all times</u>.

Discrimination is defined *'as the treatment of one employee, with certain characteristics, less favourably than another employee not having those characteristics'* that means treating every one the same, irrespective of –
- Skin colour, race, descent, nationality, ethnic origin.
- Religious or political beliefs.
- Gender, sexuality, sexual preference.
- Dress or appearance.
- Marital status, family.
- Physical health or condition, age, pregnancy.
- Mental health or any impairment.
- Industrial activities.

Harassment is the *'repeated unwelcome and unreciprocated acts or remarks which make the workplace unpleasant for the person targeted & where a reasonable person would have anticipated that these might be offensive'*; and includes any of the following -
- Being picked on, ridiculed or made fun of.
- Given a hard time over non-work events.
- Subjected to insults or taunts.
- Subjected to unwanted physical intimacy.
- Subjected to unwanted sexual activity.

- Subjected to remarks of a sexual connotation.
- Subjected to staring, leering or ogling of a person's body.
- Given unsolicited requests for sexual acts.
- Exposed to sexually explicit material – directly or indirectly (including posters, calendars etc on a lunchroom wall)

Bullying is *'unwelcome behaviour that a reasonable person would perceive as offensive, humiliating or intimidating'*; including –
- Yelling, verbal abuse, name calling.
- Making someone the target of pranks, teasing, practical jokes.
- Slandering of their work performance.
- Tampering with personal effects or gear.
- Ignoring, excluding or isolating an individual.
- Physical abuse (rough contact, pushing etc).
- Physical altercation (fighting).
- Violent menacing or making threats

Wrongful Dismissal is described as *'dismissing an employee without sufficient grounds to justify it'*

Your Business should have a written 'Behavioural Management' process that identifies how any of these breach in conduct will be handled and should include at least - Counselling, 1st Warning, 2nd Warning, Notice of Intent to Dismiss or Instant Dismissal.

Dismissal can be given for many reasons and will not (usually) be viewed as 'wrongful' if it has been the result of a process that includes each of the above steps and specifies that the penalty matches the problem.

Industrial Relations legislation breaches are a set of problems that would take months to study and then it's a fair bet you won't remember them all anyway. The shortcut is to know that these are determined by others (the government or your Company's IR advisors) and any questions need to be referred to them.

Industrial Relations rules as they relate to Your Business will be addressed in documents like an industrial award or a Workplace / Employment Contract; and should be reflected in the Behavioural Management program.

Behavioural Management Program

Your Business' Behavioural Management program must ensure information & advice is available to all employees at all times AND that they follow it AND that they are aware of their –

- ENTITLEMENT to work in a non-hostile and safe environment.

- OBLIGATION to monitor, identifying & report 'unacceptable behaviour'.

- RESPONSIBILITY to maintain a safe workplace environment at all times.

- RISK to them if they fail to comply with their obligations and responsibilities.

- EXPECTATION to (be able to) openly discuss issues before they escalate into problems.

- ACCESS to advice and guidance, at anytime it is required, including from specialist advisors.

- REQUIREMENT to follow the advice given by the specialist consultants/ advisors etc

Workplace Health & Safety is another specialist field of knowledge that you are expected to understand and apply, without having the years required to learn it. We can take some practical shortcuts in understanding WH&S legislation - let me stress that the shortcuts are in how you find the knowledge you need, not in cutting corners when applying it.

WH&S directions can be found in documents, which your business should have that define how each job is to be performed; and may include one or more of the following -

- Operator Handbook (plant, equipment, tools).
- Safe Work Instruction (job & task processes).
- Job Safety Analysis.
- Risk Assessment (identifies tasks, risks and ways to reduce them).
- Toolbox Talks (updating or awareness training on site in safe working practices).

All of these documents are designed to minimise the risk of injury or incident resulting from any workplace accident or hazard.

Applying Risk Management

In SWEAR at Your Staff we explore risk management on a personal level and learn how to apply it as a team leader, here we want to focus on the risks to Your Business and how to avoid them.

Risk Management is another way of saying that:

"A person needs the knowledge and understanding of all the processes and factors involved, to allow them to assess the situation; that will then enable them to make the right decision"

In other words Your Business must provide all employees and visitors with Risk Management guidelines - rules and procedures to follow - that will enable them to:
- Understand the processes,

- Recognise the risks and hazards; and
- Act accordingly!

Whilst Your Business should seek specialist help in drafting your risk management protocols (the forms and processes to be used); you should also understand they must –

- Be based on standards set by government legislation that requires safety to be considered in every job / task (understand the processes).

- Require a user to follow some sort of 'Hierarchy of Controls' guiding through the steps to be considered (Recognise the risk & act accordingly)

The Hierarchy of Controls appears in various formats but basically it will ask you to consider which of the following steps (best to least effective) can you apply?

1. Eliminate – completely remove the hazard
2. Substitute – hazard action for a lesser one.
3. Redesign – equipment or the work practice.
4. Separate – isolate the hazard.
5. Administer – supervision, training, process.
6. PPE – using PPE to protect personnel.

Challenge: Use this hierarchy to open a beer or sit on a chair?
A:

By the way, many of the lessons we cover in SWEAR refer the importance of understanding the situation, recognising what can go wrong and acting accordingly – so risk management is very much a part of the everyday of Your Business!

When you think about it risk management touches everything we do in business from our own wellbeing (our personal risk) to the operational activities (what can go wrong on the job and who can get hurt) to strategic risk management (what can hurt the business).

Strategic Risk Planning

The aim of the process above is to prevent (if possible) or minimise the impact of an incident.

Strategic risk management is about having a plan for what to do after the incident has occurred (ie after the above process failed to prevent it).

Your Business (and each part of it) will be affected to varying degrees by different incidents. For example it is easy to see that if your office is destroyed by fire you should have had back-ups of all key files and least some basic office equipment and space somewhere; so business can continue.

Or, that if the factory is destroyed by weather you should have a plan to outsource work to keep production going and customers satisfied?

But as catastrophic as these two events are for Your Business; surprisingly they would list as lesser events in the Risk Register for a site operation.

Similarly, the site operation may not be affected by an incident on another site, unless some equipment they were expecting to use was now not available. This event would have a more significant impact for which they would need a strategic risk plan.

Of course, preparing such a list for every part of the business a big project that may require a lot of time (which you don't have), so let's simplify it ...

Each department or team leader prepares a list of risks or potential events that concerns them and includes the proposed action they plan to take (a couple of alternatives is a good idea) AND they look at the lists of others whom they receive from, supply to or share space with.

Accordingly, they may now want to add to their original list; which of course will then be reviewed again by the others. The process can take a few loops to complete but the end result is a Strategic Risk Register for Your Business – one that covers every operational to financial risk from department to corporate etc.

Like all risk management material this Risk Register should be reviewed periodically and especially after any time it is required to be used.

12 BUSINESS MODEL
(How to make Your Business work!)

> **Challenge:** Does Your Business work effectively the way it is?
> A:

Earlier we mentioned the four functions of Your Business, as being -

- **DEMAND**
- **SUPPLY**
- **PRODUCTION**
- **CONTROL**

And how Your Business operates and structures its use of these is the '**business model**' - each of these four functions may be made up of any number of 'components' and we discussed examples of this earlier -

DEMAND –
Sales, Marketing, PR, Advertising (print, TV etc)

SUPPLY –
Goods receiving, Despatch, Delivery process (both in & out)

PRODUCTION –
Manufacture/ Service, R&D, Sub-Contracting
Warehouse/ Stores

CONTROL –
Supervision, Administration, Reporting

Rationalizing your business into small parts in this way makes it easier to understand how it works and how to improve parts of the business model.

The bad news is ... you're expected try to improve (almost) every one of these functions AND to keep on improving them year after year. This is what complicates the hell out of business management - as we (try to) keep up with all the changes in new industry techniques, social expectations & all the laws, legislations and the latest business management trends.

Have you ever thought you are doing too much OR that there is too much to do?

And so yes, business management is complicated ... if we don't understand it!

But let's take a look at each function of your business and see if we can UNDERSTAND the function better and turn it into an asset of Your Business (PAL)!

Oh by the way, remember KISS? Let's use it first on all those new business management trends ... forget them! From now on you look at them and think 'how will that fit into AND improve Your Business - now that you fully understand it?' If it doesn't fit, don't force it. You know Your Business and you know what it needs!

So what are the functions of the business and do we really only do four things?

DEMAND

This is the function where you generate and receive sales orders. It is the result of the efforts of your salespeople, advertising, promotions, publicity and word of mouth etc. It also forms the basis for the goodwill of your business (important when you come to sell it) - so you might really want to protect and develop 'demand' and you can't do that if you don't understand it.

To find out how well this function works, have a friend or spouse (or an outside agency) 'secret shop' with your business to see if they find the process (staff, details, paperwork etc) enjoyable or if doing business with you is a struggle?

If a person that is not experienced in your company struggles with your sales process then maybe your client's new purchasing officer does as well. It might be time to simplify your sales process so 'everyone' can understand it and this may lead to more sales which creates more demand; making this function a real asset.

Caution: before making changes to this function, ask first, how many extra sales are needed to 'cost justify' the change? Sometimes cost outweighs the viability of making some changes.

Elements affecting demand include – canvassing / finding customers, advertising, public relations, media coverage, customer needs (product range), negotiating skills, sales process and sales documentation.

Factors affected by and influencing changes to the process are – staff, reputation, culture, marketplace Clearly any improvement to the process that results in increased demand will benefit each of these factors.

Once you have assessed and structured these parts of your demand function the only factors that will remain out of your control are the changing circumstances caused by the marketplace.

SUPPLY

Is about delivering goods or services to your customers AND getting them from your suppliers

Do you understand how and when you deliver to each of your customers and why you do it that way? Would your customers tell you if there were any problems, or a better time or a more suitable way, unless you ask them? Or would they simply stop ordering?

Do you have this same (or a better) relationship with your suppliers?

Is your supply procedure simple and efficient or did it grow up with the business? Is the paperwork easy to use and efficient or do staff file the 3rd and 4th copies of documents? Have you discussed with your suppliers how and when you need deliveries or do you take them when THEY send them? Things change, has your supply process changed with it?

If you asked a neighbour to receive a delivery for you at their home, out of courtesy you would make sure they knew who, what and when to expect the delivery. Don't your clients deserve that same level of courtesy when you are delivering to them? And don't you deserve it from your suppliers?

Ask your staff (those involved with supply) to each re-design the supply process and paperwork to what they think will work best and then consider what they create as if you were your supplier or customer.

Staff will usually look for the simplest way to do things - maybe because they're lazy or more likely because they have to do it every day; but simple is good and often cheaper; and understanding how to make it simple will help turn the process of supply from a liability into an asset.

Factors affecting supply include – availability of materials/ products / services, transport, logistics (weather, communication) and reporting – and the requirements are exactly the same for supply from you to a client AND from a supplier to you (his client).

Factors affected by and influencing changes to the process are – staff, reputation, culture, marketplace Clearly any improvement to the process that makes supply easier, cheaper, more efficient will benefit each of these factors.

Not sure about us grouping supplies IN and supplies OUT in the same function then try delivering your product if you didn't get the materials to build it!

PRODUCTION

Production as a function is often misunderstood, even though it is the core of most businesses and it doesn't matter if you are offering a product or a service, because –

- Both require effort to produce the 'end result' and
- Both are affected by the same factors.

We tend to over-complicate Production by analysing it as a complete process rather than a series of inter-related steps ... where each step is something that can be done independent of the next or the previous step.

Let's KISS production problems good bye –
- First, we identify each of the steps that make up the process.
- Second, we study and understand each of these steps and the factors that affect it.
- Third, we examine how they interact.

Whether you provide a manufactured product or services rendered, production begins when the manpower, machinery and materials are at the workplace ready to create the 'product'. Getting them to and from the workplace is a supply function, after all who is the transport expert in Your Business?

Elements that affect production are – the process, machinery, materials, manpower and skill levels and the budget (quoted price) - all of which can be planned and are within your control.

You know (or can find out) the cost per hour of operating each piece of machinery and the cost of materials needed and labour (including on-costs) and how much they can produce each hour. So you (can) understand exactly what production costs you. And your budgets and prices should reflect this.

If on the other hand you do not know these things, or why the costs exceeded budget, or why you failed to reach production schedules, then you do not understand the production function.

Challenge: use as an example a job in production that you fully understand (one you have done) and cost it out completely – labour, machinery, materials, time required for each step; then do the same for every other job (if you don't know a job, learn it or find someone who does). Now, do all these parts equal your budget allocation for that job? If not, ask why?

If the answer is because we didn't allow for some 'unforeseen circumstances' then you are missing the point of this whole exercise; the 'unforeseen' is exactly what we are trying to identify and eliminate or provide for in our business, so ...

Challenge: List down the 'unforeseen things' that have affected production in the last six months and analyse what caused them... they will be either a failure in some other function such as Supply (address it there), or in one or more of the elements of production - machinery, material, labour or process.

Have you ever heard the saying 'Cause and Effect'?

That is what's happening here – cause and effect.

We identify the unforeseen event – but this is often just the result (the effect) of some actions. What we need to know what caused it to happen?

When we understand the cause of the problem (rather than just responding to the effect or result) we are able to better understand, handle and resolve the issues - that sounds familiar.

To find the true cause of a problem keep asking 'WHY' at each stage in the process – *why* did this happen, *why* did you do that? When you know what caused the problem at that stage (was it a response to the effect?), keep asking *why* at the next stage until you find the 'CAUSE' of the problem then you will know how to fix or eliminate it, or at least how to reduce its impact on your production function.

Factors affected by and influencing changes in production are (the usual suspects) – staff, reputation, culture, marketplace - and clearly any improvement to the process that improves production will improve each of these factors.

CONTROL

Control is what keeps every aspect of the business moving forward; it also seems to be the hardest function to get right and is **always** the last thing businessmen want to delegate or relinquish.

Every function and every factor of the business needs controls - from manpower to operations to finances to compliance with legislation, customer requirements, supply, demand, production etc - and YOU cannot be on top of all this, all of the time so some control functions have to be <u>entrusted</u> into the hands of others … or the business cannot and will not grow.

"Ok, but who should be responsible for controlling what?" and more importantly "how will I know if they are doing it right if I'm not constantly looking over their shoulder?"

The answer is you must have trust! Not *just* in your people but in the systems that will govern what they do and how they do it.

Again, let's look to understand control by looking at the two definitions of control that are relevant to YOUR business.

Control is defined as being either -
- **The apparatus by which machinery in operation is kept operating.**

- **The ability, function or power to regulate and direct activity.**

So in every function within Your Business, some people will be the -
- Machinery in operation – operators, tradesmen, labourers etc
- Apparatus by which machinery is kept operating - lead hands, foremen, supervisors.

And others will have the -
- Ability and function to regulate - Managers, Superintendents
- Power to direct (to say how it will be done) – that would be YOU!

As the head of Your Business, you have the responsibility to ensure that the business is profitable and does not fail ... and to 'regulate and direct' those persons that maintain 'the apparatus that keeps the machine in operation'.

This means your job is to 'watch over the business'; no one expects you to do everything – that's what you employ people for! In other words, they don't want you to buy a watchdog and then do your own barking ... but they do want to know that you look out the window when it barks!

When you started in business you had to control every function of the business because in those days YOU WERE responsible for demand, supply, production and control – but as we have seen, these first three functions (demand, supply and production) have all had to be allowed to develop beyond you ... and so must control.

"But control is different! How do I delegate control and still sleep at night?

13 DELEGATING
(The scariest thing you do!)

> **Challenge:** Do you delegate authority or responsibility?
> A:

Everyone will tell you, infact you probably already know, that delegating control of Your Business is scary. How will you know that person will look after things as diligently as you do?

And so what do you do? You appoint someone and then, like many business leaders, you check on what they're doing, challenge their actions and their intentions and then you wonder why they think you don't trust them!

If you have, now or in the past, been promoted to a senior position and been delegated responsibility – how did you respond? I'd say, if you're like 99 in 100 you tried damned hard to do the job, put in the extra effort and tolerated being doubted and challenged (by the boss) at every turn.

Here is a thought, the same one that you (probably) took into that job - if you employ someone with the right skills; give them the tools, materials, adequate time and clear directions of what, how, where, when and why the job has to be done, they will usually do it the best they can, just like you!

So why then, when you appoint someone do you feel the need to 'look over their shoulder'?

Maybe, it's because you don't think they are quite good enough (then why did you appoint them); or because you know that even though the job turned out well, you took shortcuts or had close calls and had to manage problems to got away with it?

In 'Message to Garcia' we identified that the ideal person to handle a job is the one who takes it on, who manages through problems etc and finds a way to get it done - someone who delivers without the need to be micro-managed.

Of course, we know we can't just give them the job and keep our fingers crossed and that is why we need supervision - to be a second pair of eyes, reducing the chance of missing mistakes. So when you appoint someone to a job and then look over their shoulder, you are supervising ... right?

Delegating is about having someone (other than you) supervising, being that second pair of eyes; someone who can control that part of Your

Business. Someone (or something) that knows what's going on …or not … in time to allow any errors to be fixed before they become a problem.

You may have already appointed people into roles where they are responsible for what goes on but have you delegated the authority to control, or are you still supervising because they are 'still earning your trust'? In other words – sure you have a watchdog but are you still doing your own barking?

Imagine in Your Business, you are responsible for all the outcomes, but what would happen if you didn't have control of the necessary functions?

Say, for example, you have to deliver a product made to set specifications by a certain date, but the customer is going to give you the instructions, or the materials to build it (when they can) or you have to use the people they say to use (and they will tell you when they're available). How do you plan or control such a job? How can you guarantee it, when you have been delegated the responsibility (for the outcomes) but not the authority (to control the functions)?

So what do you think - should you delegate just responsibility OR responsibility and control?

Delegating control is easier than you think, infact you already do it; for example you don't personally count your money every month –
1. The bank statement reports that to you;
2. Your accounts staff calculate what should be there and cross-check it to the bank statement.
3. Your accountant double checks it all as well.

So you have already delegated responsibility and control to the system and the people responsible for it, with of all things ... your money!

You don't personally go behind each salesperson to check which customers they have talked to – their sales performance report gives you that information; and you use it to judge their effort and you know it to be correct because the numbers of sales match the sales / delivery report.

Same in production, they give you a report on the quantity they have produced versus their budget or quota and a delivery report shows that this volume has been dispatched; and as a third-person check there are the invoices that confirm what has been sold and delivered.

I know this seems over-simplified, but have you noticed the trend here – REPORTS!

Reports that are delivered to you already from multiple sources that cross-check each other and confirm that things are working as planned ... or not! Reports that confirm the controls that are in place are working and monitoring Your Business.

The purpose of delegating is to free you, and other people to perform the control functions that are expected of you (and them). But delegating only works when you have systems in place that can (to your satisfaction) confirm these outcomes. You wouldn't trust just the bank statement to know how much money you have; or take the salesman's word for it, right?

So you need to build a system of reporting that gives you the information you need and the confidence to trust the people delegated to manage the systems that control Your Business.

14 USING REPORTS
(See Weekly Expense Activity Reports)

> **Challenge:** Do you know what's going on in Your Business?
> A:

We started this book by saying that the title meant Show Weekly Expense & Activity Reports and of course this means that to us reports are important. Why? Because they can and will show you how each part of the business is performing! So if you don't have reports that do this – it is time to get them!

What format you want these reports to be, how elaborate and detailed, depends on you (after all you have the power to direct) ... so long they tell you what YOU want to know ... that each part of the business is performing and the process is checking that things are operating to YOUR expectations.

There are many software packages that provide reporting systems for you, but they should come later - it is better to start with something basic (even a hand written checklist) until you know exactly what you want and need in your reporting process. I believe in incorporating technology, but don't let it hijack the process.

So how do we create a report process?

1. Write down each function, department or activity in your business and who they should report to.//2. Now list what you want to know about each one in a report – their performance results, problems, delays, labour used & expenses etc.
3. Identify how often you want to know this – daily for critical matters, weekly for production & costs, monthly for summary/ routine events.
4. Then list each factor that might affect them – the report should show how it was handled.
5. Then consider how each of these answers may be verified by another part of Your Business *and* ensure this information is covered in their report process, and if possible include a 3rd party check report (remember the bank statement exercise).
6. Lastly plan how this report information can be incorporated into the job process – as a job sheet / planning document, rather than as a "report" to be completed after work!

Once you have 'drafted' this report information into a format that YOU want to see, give it to the department heads/ team leaders and their staff to comment on so they can all have input into (and therefore ownership of) the job sheets that they will work with to show you how they are going.

As well as the report content the frequency is important - remember the aim of the report is to show what is happening in time to make any corrections that are needed, which is why I recommend at least weekly. In this way no problem can be unrecognized or uncorrected for more than a week. It is also fair to assume that if the report you want to see weekly was filled out and sent to you (or someone) every day, then any problems that showed up could be identified and acted on sooner, even daily... the ultimate in Corporate Governance!

Another home truth is that people hate having to make time to fill in those 'damned reports' – and this fact holds true for every job in your business – salesman, accounts clerk, factory hand, cleaner, general manager even managing directors – we all hate doing the paperwork!

So the best reporting systems are ones that record (and regulate) the on-going works of the business (as part of the everyday process) ... rather than ones that are presented later, as a summary of what has already happened.

"If it's that simple why doesn't everyone do it?"

Good question?

We can all see how this reporting process would work well, but we can also understand that it may take a bit of time and effort to implement; and you'll need cooperation from your team to keep it right, and perseverance to maintain it, especially when someone lets it breakdown.

It's Your Business, so it's up to you? Of course it may require some effort; but isn't it worth it to have it run smoothly and not give you headaches?

One closing thought on REPORTS, I know a businessman who, when he started out on his own, was worried that he was NOW the last line of authority (as a manager he had always had a boss to report to) and now he was IT. He worried about what happens if he didn't get it right. I suggested that he should prepare a report each month as if it were going to the board AND he should review it a week later ... this way he could correct anything he picked up on.

He took it one step further, he prepared the report and gave it to his wife to review and she challenged him on his expenses ... and so now he does have a BOSS to report to!

15 GROWING BUSINESS – Part 1: Customers
(Finding & keeping clients)

> **Challenge:** How much did your business grow last year?
> A:

Would you like to help Your Business grow? Well assuming you will make some of the changes mentioned here and you're sure it will not fail; then we have to look at two important areas of growth – CUSTOMERS and STAFF.

These two items must grow together - almost like what came first the chicken or the egg – because without new customers we don't need extra staff and without extra staff we won't keep new customers.

You know that scene in the Wild West movies with the poster on the wall - the picture of a bad looking dude and the words that say 'Wanted Dead or Alive'? Well in this scene that picture is you and the poster has been put up by your customers.

Of course you know that your competitors are trying to kill you by taking your customers (that's a story for another day) but did you know your customers also want you dead or alive?

What we're talking about here is satisfying customers because, firstly it brings in the money, and secondly we have all heard of suppliers that were dismissed because of their failure to satisfy a client's expectations.

That's the *price* on your head, if the client likes Your Business they want you alive and helping them, but if the client stops liking Your Business then they want you dead and gone.

Remember we defined Your Business as the department or team that you are responsible for? This means that your customers are the end-users of the product or service created by Your Business. This may be a business down the road or another in-house department - like the service team that uses the products that your team stores, or all those people that rely on your admin service or support advice - and keeping customers satisfied will determine if you are wanted ... dead or alive!

How can YOU guarantee customer satisfaction?

Have you ever asked a customer service or sales rep to transfer you to a more helpful person? Or have you ever decided not to go back to a restaurant or a hairdresser because you didn't get good service? In both these examples you, the customer, wanted these people dead and off you project. So you sacked them and took away their future business. Like you, your customers want to deal with only those people that work well for them and they will sack those that *fail to perform to expectation*!

Earlier we looked at *failure to perform to expectation* in our staff; we examined how to find the cause and how to handle it by motivation or discipline. But customers aren't in the position to, or even interested in teaching us how to improve. No, just as you did with the sales rep and the hairdresser, we as customers treat failure to perform with a severe penalty – we sack the offender - to us they are dead! That is why you hear of companies dismissing an errant supervisor on the 'suggestion' of a client, the alternative is they risk losing the customer if they don't.

But does this seem fair?

The answer is YES!

When we talked about the four functions of a business, one of those was DEMAND. We created the demand (having the customer wanting us) by creating the expectation of what we would do for them – and now they want it! What's more if we don't give it to them they will go with someone else who promises to deliver it. In other words the client will sack us! Remember …

We agreed to meet the customer's needs – so make sure we share these expectations with others (people or departments) in Your Business that will be involved in the process of delivering them.

We created their expectations – so take steps to make sure EVERYTHING we promised is available and can and will be delivered.

In most situations meeting the client's needs is enough to stop the client wanting you *dead* … but what happens if you are in a competitive market and the while the client doesn't want you dead, they want someone else *alive* more?

When you asked that sales or service rep to transfer you to a more helpful person, what did you hope would happen?

That you'd get someone who understood what you wanted, who knew more about the product or who would try that little bit harder to fix the problem – someone who would say "I know what you want, let me satisfy your needs?"

Customers want to be served by those businesses that don't just meet their needs but pre-empt them, that show initiative and go that little bit further for the customer; who thinks they are wonderful, and gives them more business and everyone is happy!

How to pre-empt customer's needs!

Pre-empting is probably not the right term here because we already know the customer's needs.

At some point we asked the customer what they wanted and they told us and we said we could do it for them. Actually, we probably said we <u>would</u> do it for them!

How we handled that stage of the process had a BIG bearing on our getting the work, right? At that stage the customer had high hopes that we would help them.

So now we have, at our disposal, all the tools we need to serve the customer and to pre-empt their needs:

- We have a list of what the client needs (their expectations);
- We have a list of the things that they might like (extras that were mentioned and they showed interest in);
- We have a list of things they do not like (those ideas they rejected or showed no interest in).
- We knew (from our experience) what problems we may encounter in delivering them AND

- We know (from Company expertise) what other elements should or could be considered. We may even have identified these to the client and asked what they thought about them?

We know the client's needs and what they would like to have; and we can use this knowledge to build a relationship with the client based on giving customer satisfaction!

Relationships with Customers or Clients

One of the things I often mix up (even in this book) is whether to refer to the person who buys from me as a Customer or a Client? By definition a customer is someone who buys goods or services from a business; while a client is one who uses (presumably buys) the services of a professional person or organisation. So depending on the nature of Your Business the same person could be your customer and my client. So please forgive me if I continue to inter mix the terms; but whatever you call them remember that customers or clients are people too!

When you first meet someone that you want to get to know better (to form a relationship with), what do you do?

At the beginning you take time to find out about the person (understand them). What type of character they are, what they like, what they dislike, what they know and what they might expect from a relationship? You ask questions that lead toward things you want to know about – if he is a mechanic, can he tune a (whatever you own); or as a selector of a sports team what they look for in a player; and if it is a romantic interest, what do they like to do (etc, etc).

You are looking for things about the person that will help you to understand them and that you can use to benefit your cause. This is not some nasty guide on how to *use* people – it's a natural phase in 'people relationships'. How many friends do you have that you know nothing about or with whom you have nothing in common? The answer will be nil, or very close to it. So, we need to understand about people in order to form a relationship with them, any kind of relationship.

"But I don't want to have a relationship with my customers; I just want them to buy my (widgets)?"

Really! In SWEAR at Your Customers we explore (more fully) *how* and *why* to build relationships through marketing, sales technique and after-sales service etc; but for now I want to summarise what Your Business needs to understand about customer relationships.

People will say 'yes' only when they want to! You go to the supermarket and you buy only a few of the thousands of things on offer – why? You say yes to the things you want; you don't buy soap if you don't want it this week. But you may look at a dozen brands of (widgets) and for the first time ever you chose that one – why?

Because, even though you have never used it you formed a 'relationship' with the product, built by the manufacturer's advertising which made you *want* the product (or at least to try it). And let's face it you are in that store because the store's advertising has attracted you (wider aisles, greater range etc) by creating a relationship that makes you feel better about shopping there.

Now suppose, when you go to the checkout half the registers aren't working and the queue is a mile long - you have two choices, you can wait or you can sack the store and leave without buying any widgets. If you leave the relationship with the store and the widget maker just failed.

Why do you suppose a tradesman buys his widgets from shop A and not from shop B? Both have the same products, same brands, prices, discounts etc, both have convenient locations and similar advertising that can build relationships etc. So why does the tradesman buy his widgets from shop A?

Could it be that the sales guys at shop A do that little bit extra to make the customer feel welcome, or do they find that out-of-stock product. They have a relationship with the customer – while ever they deliver this level of service (satisfying needs) the customer will *want* to keep coming back.

So before someone buys your widget something has to make them *want* it; and something has to make them want to deal with you – someone or something has to build a relationship with them.

That is *why* we need a relationship with our client - to create the **want**! The want to buy *our* product; and the want to have us – dead or alive (preferably alive)!

Relationships (good and bad) build over time based on what we do – they get the chance to start by you understanding the wants and needs of the other person (the items on the customer's want list referred to above); and they grow and prosper by how well we interact with and satisfy the other person's needs. This works both ways of course if our needs aren't satisfied we stop the relationship (we might sack a customer if he doesn't pay)

It may be worth going back to People are a Pain in the Butt, Part 2, to see the impact of personality conflicts in customer situations and how to handle them. But for now we need to consider what type of customer we are dealing with?

There are three different types of customer, and you can identify them by what they do, how it shows you what they want from you. They are –

- **The Realist** – knows what is available in the market, has researched the options and therefore can recognise and understand technical details and difficulties that you may discuss.
    - *Be straightforward and factual and work with this client to develop his project.*

- **The Dreamer** – has a vision but (possibly) limited practical knowledge of how to get it. He sees you as the 'expert' and expects you to provide the detail and guidance required.
    - *Be enthusiastic and keep this client excited about what you can do to make his dream a reality. Present variations that are needed to make project improvements.*

- **The Pretender** – thinks this is what he wants, but has no idea of getting started, let alone getting there; and he is quite happy to change the job specifications as he understands the project better. Expect delays in getting a decision as this client tries to digest all the input he receives from all the 'experts' advising him.
    - *Identify what goals this customer expects to achieve from the project and present options (no more than three) that will achieve each goal.*

- *Use this method to step the client through the project as you see it.*
- *Keep communicating with this client often (even monopolize his time to prevent others stepping in) and ensure all steps agreed to are confirmed in writing – if need be, you write and he responds.*

The old adage "The Customer is Always Right" is true, as we have seen they can even determine if you are alive or dead. But being right is based on what you know at the time – and that can change. Thomas Edison tried 10,000 things before he found what would work in a light bulb – so he must have thought he was right 10,000 times! Perhaps the adage should read "The Customer is Always right … even when he changes his mind!"

Directing Customer Expectations

Have you ever noticed how a good sales person will approach you and make it seem that your coming to him has made his day? If he said this, you'd think it a corny sales pitch but when he makes you feel that he wants to serve you and help, you become more open to his input and accepting of his capability. As a result of this *he* has a good chance to become the person you *want* to deal with!

In every form of negotiation – the sale, after-sales, each step in a project - the client may be calling the shots and may have the final say, but there will always be thing/s they has missed, or doesn't know, or an improvement they may want to adopt … be the one who presents these ideas!

Share your wisdom and experience as often as you can, be the capable one who offers input, helps the customer understand the extras that his project needs or may be improved by – and become the person he *wants* to deal with!

Start as early as you can in the process, once you understand their wants and needs, look for ways to direct their expectations. Offer suggestions!

Is their project timetable suitable? Will the tender document show them exactly what you want them to see (if you can't see it neither will they)? How will they assess the options & technical data (can you offer to consult)?

It's never too early to demonstrate to the client your professionalism and your enthusiasm for being involved.

Submitting a tender or a recommendation for example - if you're like most people you deliver the documents by the due date and then sit back and wait.

But would you accept that in Your Business?

Would you let someone start a job without having a plan showing when each stage will be completed and reported on? Hopefully the answer now is no! But how can you hold the client to this same standard?

It starts at the earliest stages of the process. When you recognise, or know from past experience, that the client may procrastinate in the evaluation stage. Perhaps this may be the result of having too many options to compare, or features and benefits to assess at one time. Whatever may cause a delay in the decision process will work against most sellers but can be made to work for the preferred operator.

Encourage the client to introduce project key points (KPI - Key Performance Indicator) if not already there – and to set up a project timetable.

A project time-table should set definite points at which progress can be measured, for example –

1) **Research** – limit the time needed to access and understand project details.

2) **Discuss options meeting** – set a date for a 1 on 1 meeting to discuss the research (give client advance notice of the results) and try to discuss them before any formal presentation is made.

3) **Assess variations** – the time required to assess any variations and to adjust the project / quote / tender requirements.

4) **Presentation / Quote** – the date may be set by client (in which case build the above timetable by working backward) or set by you (moving forwards).

5) **Decision deadline** – clients will often be vague as to when the decision will be made, but if you have been precise and professional in your dealings, meetings, KPI, dates etc then you should expect (and request) the courtesy of having a nominated deadline and having it adhered to.

6) **Follow Up** – liaise with the client as often as is practical to create a closer relationship. This is often an uncomfortable task, but if you believe in the offer you have made, that it benefits the client and Your Business then you will want every opportunity to help the client understand and appreciate the offer. Some examples of reasons to call are –

- Ensuring they got the documents.
- Understanding of the workings.
- Discuss any further details.
- Offer to view some examples of the Company's similar work.

Ownership of the idea and the extras

We talked before about keeping control of the situation and of showing your professionalism, well 'establishing the extras' is a real opportunity to do this. If you present options, advise and consult with the customer - then these extras or variations will become part of the package (that you helped build), project requirements in the quote / tender - giving you an edge, because you know exactly how and why to present them.

Have you ever noticed that there are almost always extras (after thoughts) added onto the project? This is because someone is helping YOUR client to 'better understand' their project and getting to alter or add what THEY want.

Someone is stealing your client! So if you're not calling the shots then it is costing you work!

The client (whatever type they are) wants their project to be the best ever and they will listen to improvements and suggestions; they may not give you credit in the process but you can be assured they will be grateful.

Just remember to make sure they want YOU and your team contributing to its success!

15 GROWING BUSINESS – Part 2: Staff
(Finding & keeping staff)

> **Challenge:** How much did your staff numbers grow last year?
> A:

Keeping constant growth in Your Business is not easy, firstly you don't know exactly when new customers or new orders are going to appear and secondly, you don't know if you'll be able to find new staff when you need them. That is why we must try to grow these two items together.

In SWEAR at Your Staff we have explored the role of the team leader in ensuring that the quality of new employees is in step with the needs and expectations of the business – here we must look at what Your Business should do to support this.

Those responsible for recruiting new staff should have a *'shopping list'* of the things that the business and team wants in a new employee, such things as –

- Skill set – what talents they should have?
- Experience – What experience you consider mandatory for the position?
- Personality - Is the team they'll be working in a serious or a fun-loving crew?
- Mind set – How does this position match the applicant's expectations?
- Is it a stepping stone or a career highpoint?
- Enthusiasm – How much do they want this job, and why?

We must also remember that the labour market (ie, availability of job applicants) will vary from time to time – ranging from plenty of people to chose from to shortages of skilled labour.

The impact of this is that in so called 'employer good times' we are more demanding of the skills and experience we accept; but as times change so do our expectations because we need people in those jobs; and we progressively alter our criteria for assessing applicants. Ultimately, we are likely to be selecting lesser quality persons to jobs.

This can have the effect of downgrading accepted performance standards within Your Business as newer employees who cannot meet the standards struggle to deliver to the expectations of those who were employed into similar positions before.

What do you think this will do for morale?

Certainly, older established employees will feel that they are expected to give more than newer employees, or alternatively newer staff may feel that too much is expected of them. Either scenario is not good for Your Business.

One way to avoid this situation, in both good times and bad, is to include in the recruitment mix the element of 'enthusiasm' –
- Why does the person want this job?
- How does this job fit into their career ambition?
- What should we demand of, and expect to get from this applicant?

In this way, even if skill level or experience is discounted (or diluted), you can still rely on mind-set and enthusiasm as constant factors in the recruitment decision-making process.

Replacing a team member is always difficult.

Everyone feels the pain of replacing staff even the new guy, because if the outgoing worker was –
- Good – he leaves big shoes to fill; it's harder for the newbie to offer ideas or improvements.
- Not so good – he leaves the job in a mess which creates more work to get back on track.

Keeping Staff

It is a well documented fact that it costs three times as much to recruit and train a new starter than it does to keep the old one. And guess where most of that expense occurs? Yep, in your supervisor's time - helping them to get settled in, trained and up-to-speed; taking time and focus away from their core role of controlling their team and the works.

We all know some workers make it impossible to keep them, but let's concentrate on the others, those 99% that we'd really rather keep than lose.

The two most common reasons people give for leaving a job are –
* Being UNDER APPRECIATED – they didn't recognise my effort / results.

* Being OVERWORKED – I did more than anyone else.

Keeping staff is about understanding, motivating and rewarding them. I don't mean a monthly pep talk, a quarterly review, an annual pay rise, and a night out at Christmas - because putting it like that; it doesn't sound like much of an offer, does it?

Keeping staff goes right to the heart of what we have been talking about –
* Understanding what makes them tick (what they need and want).

- Working with them to help them achieve it.

Of course we cannot always control the decision of a team member to leave, but we *should* have a damn good try!

In spite of the reasons people give for leaving, and assuming we disregard the person who wins the lottery, there are really only three reasons why people will change jobs.

What got them to *start thinking* about leaving was - the three 'Ds' (Disinterested, Disillusioned or Distracted) – after all, there must be something they stopped liking about the job?

But what made them *decide to act* and what benefits do they hope to get from making a move?

If we can understood these causes we can use them to (maybe) reverse the person's decision OR better still we could build a team spirit that people won't want to leave in the first place.

The three (3) reasons most often quoted by people for quitting a job are -

More reward – unfortunately if you can't or won't match the difference you might lose a good worker. BUT reward is only one of the reasons staff resign and surprisingly, it is not the major reason people change jobs. So it's probably not the underlying cause of their discontent. After all there had to be a reason they went looking for a new job in the first place; and found that they could earn more. Find and fix the real reason and they just might stay!

Career opportunity – is a major motivator of people who are career driven, and if you have been discussing career options regularly with the team member and helping them develop their career you will be in a position to either -

- Explain (honestly) why this is not a good opportunity for them to take up, or

- Recognise that it is, and help them exit with an 'open door to come home' at any time.

This means they may come back at any time if the new offer isn't what they expected or in the future they can apply for a new position in Your Business that is in keeping with the skills / qualifications they will have achieved – either way it is a win for Your Business.

Lifestyle – is a major reason for resigning and it is something you can control; and it starts well before the person offers their resignation. Your Business should –

- ***Encourage discussion about lifestyle pursuits*** and out-of-work interests between yourself and team members and help them identify and discuss any Work / Lifestyle conflicts.

- *Avoid roster changes* that may cause staff to have to change their days off (as much as possible). They joined Your Business on the offer to work certain days and at that time they assessed how this position would fit in their life and accepted your offer based on that. So ask yourself (or them) would they have accepted the job to work on the days you are now expecting them to work?

Note: They might accept the change for NOW, out of courtesy / necessity / fear or whatever; but if this change doesn't suit their lifestyle you can bet they will be looking for a new job.

- *Flexible work hours* (if possible) to accommodate lifestyle activities such as the occasional long weekend, a day off (with or without pay) for non-work reasons. Letting people work a little longer to 'bank' hours is a great motivator for staff and a real way in which you can assist their work and lifestyle to fit together.

Keeping staff is really about how the position fits their life now and in the future as their lifestyle and work ambitions change. For example, you have asked Fred to start working Saturdays and he said yes; but six months later he wants to join the local football team and they play on Saturdays. At that time what options does Fred have – can he change rosters, or change duties, or does he have to change employers?

Improving lifestyle has always been a major reason in why people change jobs, even careers. In the early days of the industrial revolution people moved from the farms to cities looking for jobs that improved their lifestyle (more money, less hours, better job security).

Now-a-days we might see the reverse as a better option (moving back to rural areas) but still that we recognise just like our grandfathers and those before them, that people will change to find ways to improve their lifestyle.

16 KEEPING A BUSINESS
(Secrets of owning a business)

> **Challenge:** Does your business operate to budget ?
> A:

We understand that the goals of the business are to make sales, income and then profits; and everyone accepts that this is reasonable because we all want our employer to be profitable - so we keep our job.

But how many people understand about all that secret boss stuff - like budget versus actual, forecasting, pre-tax net gains before dividends!?

Do you understand, and can you explain what goes on 'behind the scenes' of a business, what really makes it tick? Who wants to know how to explain what Your Business is really all about?

I am sorry to have to say this but … it's always about the money!

Even the most charitable of organisations needs money to survive, just like you and me; and in that way the business is very much like the family household – and knowing this helps us understand what goes on; and why the boss sometimes does things that people may not understand.

Have you ever overspent the family budget?

What did you do when you realised that you had a 'cashflow shortage' - *that's what it's called in business school* – I'm guessing you what we all do - decided to defer paying <u>some</u> bills until next payday. You had to keep some cash to make sure you could cover other things, like, money for food, to get to work, money for kids and some money just in case!

Your Business is the same - every week you have to prioritise how to spend what money comes in because you know you to keep some money for things that must get paid … like wages.

In the family budget you have one, maybe two incomes; and you know how much and when you will get paid (weekly, fortnightly, etc) – so you can plan what and when to spend. BUT imagine if you had not 2, but 3 or 4 or 10 or 20 employers all paying you their share of your weekly wage; and you didn't know exactly when they are going to pay it or even if they will pay you the full amount every time … OUCH!

This is what the business is faced with every month; and why some of the 'profit' has to be kept available to top-up cashflow when needed.

Imagine if when you go for a new job interview or a salary review, that the employer could ask you to show them all your expenses (mortgage, school fees, car payment, utilities, entertainment etc) and then says that they will pay you that amount plus a reasonable extra amount on top (the profit) for doing the job.

Again, this is exactly what a business faces – they are allowed to price their product or service to recover expenses, plus make a reasonable profit. A business that tenders for work has to present such a breakdown in writing; while a business selling in a retail market must be competitive – in both cases their price must reflect their costs (expenses) plus a reasonable profit. If they make this profit and therefore the price too high, what happens? They get no sales!

If your wages were determined in this way you would really have to watch the family budget, wouldn't you? You'd have to plan ahead for <u>all</u> expenses - buy only what you planned to buy and not overspend on the weekend. And I bet you'd start checking really close the price of everything you buy and why you need it and probably get angry at any unnecessary waste. Hey, you're starting to sound like the boss!

Money in a business is just like money in your family household (assuming that you have many employers and you don't know when or if you'll get paid or how much) and all those bills for the business, just like at home, still have to get paid and hopefully on time. Thank god for the profits you make! It allows you to top up your cashflow.

By the way, did I mention that for most businesses that profit is usually somewhere between 5% and 10% (after allowing for taxes etc) so in real terms for every $1,000 the business charges they'll make $50 - $100 in profit!

I'll bet right now you're thinking … 'if I make $1,000 a week would I be happy saving only $50?'

Welcome to the world of the business owner!

Oh, and let's not forget what happens if one of your kids quits, I don't mean grows up and leaves home, I mean quits (to join another family) and you have to replace him - although I can't think why you would want to, but let's say you do. This new kid will probably be more expensive, s/he may want more pocket money (to join your family), may have different hobbies (that you'll have to pay for). I mean you're still paying off the last kid's golf clubs and now you're going to be buy a pony, riding gear and lessons.

You probably didn't plan for this 'new kid' in your family budget, but you need him and you don't want to disappoint him by saying that he can't have his horse. So you know that somehow you'll have to sell the old kid's golf clubs to pay for the new kid's gear, horse etc; and meanwhile the rest of your family will just have to tighten up and spend less to make room for the new kid.

Remember this example when the boss asks you to justify a new purchase or to look at ways to make cost savings – it's probably being driven by the need to pay for 'a new idea that replaces someone else's earlier new idea' or for some 'new kid' in another part of the business – either way, your efforts are needed to help make this possible!

Hopefully this helps you understand (and use these examples when explaining to staff) that the business is probably not a bottomless pit of money, and the boss is probably not tightening the screws just to buy a new car or boat, infact according to statistics -

- 74% of all SME (Small Medium Enterprises) operate on negative cashflow – that is they use leases to finance the business growth and / or bank overdrafts to bridge those cashflow shortages; and

- 79% of all SME will not make any clear (of debt) profit until they sell or close the business, at which point they'll receive income without having bills to pay (remember most business are paid on invoices 30 days in arrears).

Last thing, and this is a 'sad and scary' reality - most businesses that collapse (or go broke) also take with them all the 'assets' of the business owner – the house, the cars, the toys etc. That's because most of the assets, those things that we see as symbols of success are often leased, on hire purchase or are being paid for by the business cashflow rather than profit (remember there's only so much you can do on $50 per every $1,000).

This last point should in no way detract from your impression of the boss or of the integrity of his business; after all he has built a considerable enterprise while faced with all the issues we have discussed. Nor should it be a cause for concern about the viability of the business. Based on what we have seen, if the business is paying its wages and bills regularly then the boss probably has his 'behind the scenes' dynamics working well.

What this is meant to show you is that the business operates just like your family – its budget at times is tighter than other times; it probably makes major purchases using bank loans or borrowed money (just as you would use a credit card) and it relies on all the 'family members' to do their part the best way they can to keep expenses down so it can make ends meet, and keep moving forward and supporting people like you!

You may even want to get up, go over, shake your boss's hand and say thank you! He won't understand why but I'm sure he'd appreciate it!

17 GROWING YOURSELF
(Make time and a better you!)

> **Challenge:** Are you doing exactly what you want to be doing?
> A:

I have over the years talked to many business leaders who were striving to learn more about how to run their business better, but often don't know that they needed to improve their personal skills.

When you are the boss, you are the boss and those that work for you often accept (whether they like it or not) many of the things you do and say. And while it may be appropriate for a mate on the golf course to tell you to "pull your head in" I doubt you will ever hear it in the office (unless you can read minds). So how do you learn what you need to know about YOU and how do you improve those things when you do?

In SWEAR at Your Staff (because it is about team leadership) we explore YOU on many levels and it may be valuable for you, as a leader, to review that information. What I want to do here is give you a snapshot of things you should know and a short awareness study of what they involve.

KNOWING YOURSELF

Ask yourself, what is it that makes a good leader, someone whom others want to follow? As business owner or manager you are in this role – and you have to fulfil it to everyone's expectations.

Leadership is about **UNDERSTANDING** the human side of the business - of understanding what works and why; about showing **COMPETENCE** of knowing the job - what it needs and when; and understanding the questions and the answers and having the **CONFIDENCE** to deliver them in an effective and professional manner.

PUBLIC SPEAKING

Public speaking, addressing a group, even a one on one meeting is scary for many people, especially those not comfortable in the role of a presenter.

But socially you can talk to your friends and they accept you the way you are, so by all accounts your friends must think you present ok!

Without sounding boorish, in SWEAR at Your Staff we set out a program to help you develop from friendly guy to public speaker.

What Your Business needs from you is the ability to present and share information to people (be it an audience or an audience of 1) with confidence and clarity ... to sell the message and have others follow – because that's what leaders have to do.

When giving a speech talk as yourself, like you believe in what you are saying, use words that you want to use, as you would with your friends (because that's what you want your audience to be); and remember your audience isn't there hoping that you will fail, they're hoping to be entertained, informed and/ or inspired.

The following is an extract from experts in the field - nine steps to making the perfect speech!

1. Be prepared – write it out and practice.
2. Know what you want to say - your objective.
3. Know how you want to say it – plan emotions.
4. Read as little as possible – plan use cards.
5. Visualise your success – the 1st few minutes
6. Avoid apologising - if you miss it, say it later.
7. Speak in a clear well paced voice.
8. Keep your speech going forward
9. Realise that people want you to succeed

USING TIME

Time management experts say that to understand our time usage patterns we must consider these three areas –
- Day-to-day use of your time
- Business time allocation
- Lifestyle (activities) time

Day-to-day chaos!

In business most of us can justifiably filling in our day with all the very important things we have to do … right? But still we never have enough hours and we complete the required work 'just in time to make the deadline'; and herein lays the secret – the deadline! Some people live and work with deadlines, their lives depend on them (journalist, surgeons, pilots etc) – how do they do it?

Try creating a TODO list for all the things you have to do – not just for today but make it ongoing and keep adding to it every task that you have to do. I keep mine on a clipboard on my desk (if it was on my computer I would be tempted not to look at it or update it often enough)

This way you will finish tasks before the due date not after it AND it will enable you to continually look at what's ahead and to see IF you can handle or should delegate each new task as it comes in.

Who is watching the shop?

The second part of time management is how much time you and others spend on running the business.

Create a spreadsheet showing how much (%) each person's time is spent on the following activities:
- IN – internal reports, monitoring, staff, admin
- ON – strategies, planning, training etc
- FOR – production, manpower, equipment etc
- OUT – marketing, sales, customer service, public relations, client meetings etc.

Look for changes YOU can make to your work allocation then ask others to do the same; and review this chart periodically, as this will keep increasing both productivity and efficiency.

Time Sharing – Your Business or your life!

The third part of time management is the amount of time we spend 'working' instead of with family and social or recreational activities.

I can almost guarantee that some readers will not understand this as they can justify the time spent on their career as - building a better life for the family – (wait for it) that's the same family they do not spend enough time with! I know this because I, like every older business manager has done the same thing. Would it help if I reminded you that your job is your job, not your life! OR that Your Business will survive after you, even if you don't!

Unfortunately, it usually takes a life-scare (health, family etc) to bring this work/ family ratio into a better perspective, but let's take a look at anyway.

How we plan to spend our time and how we actually do it are often not the same; and while you may know you don't have time for some activities and you 'make time' for others - do you really know how much time you are losing? Sometimes just quantifying this helps us to see more clearly what we are doing. In the table below fill in the amount of time you would like to have for each activity in the 'Wish List' column; then write in the 'Reality' column what you really do.

Lifestyle Hours Table:

Activity by Hours per Week	**Wish List**	**Reality**
Sleeping (average 7 days)		
Health & Fitness		
Leisure – Hobbies & Sport		
Family		
Domestic & Other duties		
Entertaining & Friends		
Education & Learning		
Working – ON Your Business		
Working - IN Your Business		
Total Hours per week		

Note: Total hours per week cannot exceed 168

Now you know how you spend your time each week, what you want to do and what you **are** doing – is IT the lifestyle you want to have?

SOLVING PROBLEMS

The answers you give to questions will be taken as 'your advice' and someone is going to act on it ... if it works, great ... if it doesn't, you're going to have to explain the disaster that you just created ... or worse, imagine if someone gets hurt?

If you know the answer from past experience - give it; if you do not – shut up!

Find out when they need to know the answer (their deadline) and promise (and actually do) get back to them with the correct answer in time.

This gives you time to -
- Assess the problem.
- Consider the cause and effects of the problem.
- Discuss the problem with others who have more experience in the matter.

As a result, when you do respond (before that deadline) your answer will be (more likely to be) correct and you will present it with more confidence because you are basing it on proven prior experience.

Remember: people will judge your skill by the correct advice you give, not the speed with which you give it.

REPORT WRITING

Another area of stress for many a business owner/manager is writing correspondence and reports. Of course those that work in larger organisations may have people who 'spin' this for them; but if not it is worth understanding some of the basic rules to follow.

Again we explore this more fully in SWEAR at Your Staff (you really should buy and read a copy) but the essence of what Your Business needs you to know is -

The formality of letter writing has changed over the years such that it is now acceptable (except in some legal applications) to express your thoughts as you would in a one-on-one conversation (keeping it polite of course).

There are times when a professionally drafted letter is the better way to go – when the outcome may cost Your Business money or opportunity – and in these instances 'having a go' might prove costly.

In general correspondence matters you should consider who you are writing to, what you want to say and express it (in words) as you would want it said to you.

There are many books that can help you improve you writing skills but one of the easiest ways – particularly with regards to selecting the format and layout - is to look at letters and reports written by other people and identify the style and features that you want to include in your own writing.

PS: it is not plagiarism to copy someone's layout, just don't do it in a letter back to them. I once had a client who was 'told' by a newer business in his industry to change his quote pad layout because they looked the same. I'll let you guess what the new chum was told.

MAKING YOUR MARK

We all want respect - from our peers, the team, the clients ... that good looking person next door!

But in business, as in life we will only get respect, when we have earned it.

Too often leaders 'expect' this too soon or they forget they have to earn it – "I'm the boss, so do as I say!" And what happens, they don't get respect.

We have talked earlier about company culture and the importance of developing the right attitude ... so how does the scene above fit in? It doesn't.

As a leader, how you conduct yourself will impact on the people that report to you and your attitude will affect the *culture* in Your Business.

As a generalisation, do you agree that most people want to work in a small team or enterprise, where they feel comfortable, accepted and where their efforts are recognised?

It may not surprise you to hear then, that most people expect a small business or partnership to have a better culture than a business employing many staff – the logic being that the partners will be more co-operative and more team-motivated, more result oriented, than say a salaried manager in a large organisation. This is not always true, but this is the perception that most people have of the cultures that exists in these types of businesses.

Is smaller really better?

Does being an owner or a manager in Your Business make you look differently at how you handle staff, at the things you do and the way you do them? Why?

Is it because you are a stakeholder - with a vested interest in the success of the business? And how your team performs affects your personal success?

Stakeholders are those who stand to gain from the business' success and lose from its failure.

So what sort of culture do YOU have in Your Business; and what impact is it having?

Do your team members see themselves as being stakeholders with a vested interest in the success of the business OR as just a part of the process, working for the boss?

Are they self motivated or led by carrots (incentives, bonuses etc) or kicks? Do they see their long term future with Your Business?

Much of what you have read here should help you find the answers to these questions; and to develop the right culture for Your Business and to be the leader you want to be (with or without respect).

But we all have to be what we are; we have to live with (and work on) our strengths and our weakness and as leaders we all come in different shapes and sizes and in many types and sometimes we are angry, other times nice … after all you can't be a total 100% bastard all of the time, you must have some nice features.

And like everybody you have you good days and your bad (mood swings), which unfortunately all impact on Your Business.

So, along with everything else you have to remember, you must be mindful of the mood YOU are in when dealing with business matter.

When you're in a good mood you'll get the message across right! But in a bad mood … well, who knows!?

For example, would you try and sell a million dollar deal if you're in a bad mood … I think not!

So why would you try to motivate or discipline an employee while you're in a bad mood?

And let's face it, you probably wouldn't give them a pay rise or fair hearing on that (moody) day anyway, would you? …

So, if possible put off doing things that need your total fairness until you are at a better time or day.

Do this and you will definitely make a positive mark on Your Business!

19 FINAL THOUGHTS
(Managing Your Business can be fun!)

> **Challenge:** Do you now think differently about Your Business?
> A:

The art of managing a business is about combining people (all doing their jobs); in the various functions of the business (demand, supply, production & control) to produce the product or service (result) required by the customers.

The role of the owner or manager is to direct the business, to be confident that everything is going according to plan (controls, reports etc) and to share this confidence with employees, customers and other stakeholders.

Recognise that problems will occur when people lose focus (we mentioned disinterested, disillusioned, distracted) or if they forget how or when to do something, or if requirements or expectations are changed, without giving new instructions.

This is why every business benefits from having … pre-set controls - **guidelines** (or instructions) for every function and factor, every person's job and every task within the business; somewhere that new employees (and forgetful ones) can refer to; somewhere that the business can list how, where, when, why and by whom things are to be done.

Remember we talked earlier about getting woken up in the middle of the night; and how it may be avoided by having these pre-set guidelines. We also talked about you costing every aspect of the jobs in production – well, creating guidelines or Job Role Descriptions, is a practical way of breaking every job into measurable tasks… that you can use for understanding and costing the job.

Make sure that the Job Role Description covers all parts of the job and that JRD's do not overlap, unless they should. I once found two people doing the same job an hour apart - the second person admitted the job was easy, adding "he had virtually nothing to do".

So it is good business to take the time to create instructions for every function and every task and everything that can go wrong in a job … which … means ALL of it!

Once while discussing a need to UNDERSTAND the business and apply controls I had an owner say "but we're not BHP (the then largest business in Australia) you know" and yet, while his business may have had less employees, it had almost as many job tasks and functions (demand, supply, production & control) as the 'big one'. But it was his business and his profits to protect … or not. As a side note, today his business is a national leader in his market … and yes he has set up the controls!

It's a case of *'You can lead a horse to water, but you can't make him drink!'* … which is another way of saying what was said earlier … everything you have heard today, will help you … when YOU see the need for it … when you understand how and when to apply it! The important point is that when you do it, do it right the first time so that it will prevent the matter from becoming a problem again in future.

YOU can simplify your business and you can do it your way, by –
- **UNDERSTANDING** your business,
- **KEEPING IT SIMPLE**,
- Using **PAL** to measure it and project it forward,
- Using **GUIDELINES** to regulate it,
- **DELEGATING** people to monitor the progress & performance,
- Using **REPORTS** to **control** what's going on – as it happens!

In closing, I want to say that business, like life, should be fun - enjoy the highs and lows, the buzz of success and the uncertainty of tomorrow.

But try and keep the work/ life balance; after all, even as a business owner the work you do is still 'just your job'. Look for, no, *find* ways to streamline what has to be done by you, and whenever possible delegate responsibility and control so you can make time to enjoy your business and its rewards, after all you've earned it!

If you would like further help, or to offer comments (we welcome feedback) or for more information about this or any of the SWEAR at Your Business series of books please contact the author at: ray@RayPedersen.net
or visit www.RayPedersen.net

20 BUSINESS NEEDS QUIZ
(Analysing the needs of Your Business)

> **Challenge:** Do you know what Your Business needs?
> A:

The following quiz is designed to help you analyse the needs of Your Business – to help identify its strengths, weaknesses and vulnerabilities.

If Your Business is Company/ corporate entity complete a separate analysis for each department/ branch etc and analyse each separately, because the success of Your Business depends on the combined efforts of other (team leaders) Businesses.

Your Business Needs Analysis

© 2008 RayPedersen.net

Instructions:
Your Business (YB) means the part of the entity that you control
You means you personally and/ or your specific delegates.
Score each line: 0 (No / poor) 1 (Adequate) 2 (Yes / excellent)

1 Production / Operations	0	1	2
A: Purchasing			
Are your suppliers all reliable & reasonably priced?			
Does YB have purchasing approval programs in place?			
Is there a product / supplier criteria/ selection program?			
Does YB have an established re-order procedure?			
Do you review products/ suppliers regularly?			
B: Inventory			
Does YB effective inventory control procedures?			
Are they aligned to production requirements?			
Are they followed all the time?			
Are parts 'ordered in error' managed/ returned?			
Is slow moving stock managed/ rotated/ returned?			
C: Scheduling			
Does YB plan start & end & dates for jobs?			
Do you know how long each job should take?			
Use KPI (Performance Indicators) for each stage?			
Use production planning & control tools/ docs?			
Production flows smoothly / no tie-ups or delays?			
D: Quality Control			
Does YB have a Quality Assurance procedure?			
Your Business does well in quality assessments?			
Have a 'Check & Correct' type follow-up system?			
Are inferior materials returned to suppliers?			
Are product/ services assessed with customers?			
E: Research & Development			
YB culture encourages creativity & innovation?			
Are products/ services technically competitive?			

Are R&D facilities, tools, staff etc adequate?			
Are enough new/ improved products developed?			
Are R&D time, costs & info-sharing appropriate?			
F: Workshops, Offices & Support Facilities			
Does YB have well presented facilities/ equip?			
Are support facilities accessible to project/ works?			
Do facilities meet or exceed future requirements?			
Does YB meet/ exceed industry safety standards?			
Does YB regularly review facility/ equip needs?			
G: Risk Management & Insurances			
Does YB conduct risk assessment for all works?			
Does YB conduct Strategic Risk Assessments?			
Does YB maintain a Risk Register?			
Are all potential financial risks insured?			
Are insurance policies reviewed/ tendered yearly?			
H: Information Technology Systems			
Does YB gather & share information effectively?			
Are YB staff able to access relevant information?			
Are YB staff able to input relevant information?			
Is information system secure & user friendly?			
Is info system maintained & training provided?			
Production/ Operations Score:	/80		

2 Manpower	0	1	2
A: Hiring			
Does YB have right mix of people in key roles?			
Do Vacancy ads attract appropriate applicants?			
Does YB have procedures for recruiting staff?			
Do you reference check prospective employees?			
Do team leaders offer input on job requirements?			
B: Training			
Does YB provide induction & job-skill testing?			
Do you have written Job Role Descriptions/ JRD?			

Are JRD reviewed to meet changing job needs?			
Does YB provide job improvement training?			
Does YB monitor industry trends for job reviews?			
C: Communications			
Does YB involve employees in decision making?			
Do you provide employees with clear directions?			
Do you involve employees in setting own goals?			
Do employees have access to relevant procedures?			
Do staff have a process to comment on directions?			
D: Motivating People			
Does YB have a higher than liked staff turnover?			
Do you know if employees like their job & YB?			
Do you know what motivates each employee?			
Do you discuss reason with departing employees?			
Are you confident of success at motivating staff?			
E: Disciplining People			
Does YB have a procedure for disciplining staff?			
Does YB maintain a record in personnel files?			
Do you know that all staff are aware of rules etc?			
Do you investigate the causes before disciplining?			
Are you confident of success disciplining staff?			
F: Behavioural Management			
Does YB have formal behavioural procedures?			
Does YB have clear guidelines for handling staff?			
Does YB maintain a record in personnel files?			
Do you know staff behavioural responsibilities?			
Do you know that all employees are also aware?			
G: Enforcing Policy			
Does YB conduct staff performance reviews?			
Do team leaders discuss these with employees?			
Do you check these reviews & question findings?			
Does YB use PER for promotion/ training needs?			
Does someone conduct a PER on you?			

H: Succession Planning			
Does YB have a Manpower Management chart?			
Do staff know where they fit & report to?			
Do all Team Leaders groom an understudy?			
Do you monitor the progress of all understudies?			
Do you have an understudy for your position?			
Manpower Score:		/80	

3 Sales & Marketing	0	1	2
A: Pricing			
Does YB price its product/ services appropriately?			
Does YB base prices on "cost plus" structure?			
YB prices are - top (score 1)/ bottom (0)/ mid (2)			
YB reviews "price-cost" - yearly (1)/ quarterly (2)			
YB offers effective discount to secure new work?			
B: Customer Service			
Does YB consider customer service a priority?			
Does TB have a complaints evaluation procedure?			
Does YB seek & respond to customer feedback?			
Do you handle complaints effectively?			
Have complaints decreased in last year?			
C: Sales Management			
Does YB have an effective sales force/ process?			
Does YB set & monitor individual sales targets?			
Are sales teams well managed & remunerated?			
Does YB provide sales & after-sales training?			
Does YB have minimal turnover of sales staff?			
D: Advertising & Public Relations			
Does TB have an advertising/PR			
Does YB have promotions / issue press releases?			
Does advertising budget match planned growth?			
Is advertising consistent with product & market?			
Can YB measure sales growth by source, ads/ PR?			

E: Market Research	0	1	2
Does YB identify with customer wants/ needs?			
Do you know market perception of your products?			
Do you identify target markets & growth areas?			
Has YB identified how to reach target markets?			
Do you know key differences with competitors?			
F: Marketing Planning			
Does YB have a marketing plan (1) / budget (2)?			
Does YB review plan yearly (1) / quarterly (2)?			
Does YB have a person directing marketing?			
Does marketing capitalise on market perceptions?			
Do you know how marketing differs to competitor			
Sales & Marketing Score:		/60	

4 Management

A: Strategic Management	0	1	2
Does YB have a published mission/ vision?			
Does YB have an organisational structure?			
Do procedures endorse strategic planning?			
Do employees understand/ contribute to planning?			
Does YB culture reflect & encourage the above?			
B: Recordkeeping			
Does YB store works records for required time?			
Does YB store transaction records for req time?			
Does TB store & restrict access personnel records			
Are records stored securely & easy to locate/ find?			
Does YB have document handling procedures?			
C: Decision Making Process			
Does YB have a formal decision-making process?			
Do you involve subordinates in decision-making?			
Do you give clear decisive instruction/ answers?			
Do you involve others in brain-storming sessions?			
Do you involve teams in idea generating sessions?			

D: Problem Solving Process			
Does YB have a formal problem solving process?			
Do you encourage initiative in problem solving?			
Do you offer alternative answers for consideration			
Do you always appropriate answers to problems?			
Are any unresolved problems affecting production			
E: Government Regulations			
Does YB comply with all laws & regulations?			
Does YB actively monitor changes in regulations?			
Does YB have a Compliance Register?			
Does YB monitor compliance of suppliers?			
Does YB confirm compliance renewals to clients?			
F: Leadership & Subordinates			
Does YB provide clear instruction for all activities			
Does YB have this info readily available to all?			
Do you know how to find info for all activities?			
Do you agree with all info for all activities?			
Does YB have a review process for this info?			
G: Business Law			
Does YB have advisors for legal, safety, IR?			
Do you understand all business & contract laws?			
Do you know which laws may affect YB?			
Does YB provide training in contract laws, regs?			
Do you know how subordinates keep up-to-date?			
H: Dealing with Professionals			
Does YB use external consultants, accountants?			
Do you know how well they understand YB?			
Do you understand how to apply advice provided?			
Do professionals meet with relevant subordinates?			
Do you review services, function, costs, etc?			
Management Score:		/80	

5	Financial & Accounting	0	1	2

A: Financial Analysis & Procedures		
Does YB have a strong working capital/ cashflow		
Does YB show cash growth over last 2 periods?		
Does YB produce a month-by-month budget?		
Can you understand/ read budget & balance sheet		
Does YB have good creditor, bank relationships?		
B: Bookkeeping & Accounting		
Does YB have appropriate bookkeeping systems?		
Does YB have competent in-house accounts staff?		
Do you have access to all fiscal/ accounts records?		
Do you see reports – cashflow, income, expenses?		
Do you check/ audit the accuracy of these reports?		
C: Budgeting		
Does YB set appropriate, realistic financial goals?		
Does YB operate to a monthly cashflow budget?		
Does YB use budget controls for all purchases?		
Do you see reports in time for corrective action?		
Do you involve subordinates in budget/ correction		
D: Cost Control		
Does YB manage cost of purchases in a budget?		
Does YB budget provide for capital purchases?		
Do you use the budget as a cost control tool?		
Can staff access & understand cost control tools?		
Are cost control procedures working effectively?		
E: Credit Control		
Does YB have an accounts credit procedure?		
Does YB receive payments within agreed terms?		
Does YB use account factoring to increase cash?		
Do you know collection cost of overdue accounts?		
Do you regularly review status of accounts?		
F: Raising Money		
Does YB have access to raising short-term capital		
Does YB have access to raising long-term capital?		

Do you compare cost (interest) with profit ratio?		
Are interest rates & loan conditions appropriate?		
Do you assess loan access & conditions regularly?		
G: Dealing with Banks & Financial Institutions		
Does YB use more than 1 bank/ financial provider		
Do you have good (open, friendly) relationship?		
Do you have direct access to senior executives?		
Do you involve subordinates in bank dealings?		
Do you monitor market trends of your banks?		
H: Use of Analytical Tools		
Does YB use cashflow projection analysis tools?		
Does YB use monthly P&L reporting?		
Does YB use project specific P&L reporting?		
Do you review & understand these reports?		
Do relevant subordinates review the above?		
Financial & Accounting Score:		/80

6	Your Business Needs Analysis Summary		
Production / Operations		%	/80
Manpower		%	/80
Sales & Marketing		%	/60
Management		%	/80
Financial & Accounting		%	/80
Overall		%	/380

Summary
1. The above indicates areas of strength, weakness &/or vulnerability you should check within Your Business.
2. Review each topic and question to identify those areas of most concern and address them first by -
    - Understanding the process
    - Systemising/ planning the process
    - Application & changes to the process
    - Measuring progress & development

www.ingramcontent.com/pod-product-compliance
Lightning Source LLC
Chambersburg PA
CBHW051523170526
45165CB00002B/577